A War on Friendly Grounds

By

Carlos Martin

A War on Friendly Grounds

ISBN 978-0-578-43928-0

Edited by Carolyn Billups
Author photo of Carlos Martin by Nogen Beck

Dedication

I want to dedicate this book to my family, especially my sons Jaquell and King.

A War on Friendly Grounds

Carlos Martin

Acknowledgements

I want to thank my Queen Ashli for pushing me to do the book, for challenging me and making me a better man. Thank you CEO Space family, Uncle Berny and September Dohrmann for just loving me. I truly appreciate you sharing Goddess La Hottie (Myrna Whitt) with me because she helped me out of a dark place. Byron Nelson thank you for being a beacon of light and Les Brown for allowing me to be a part of your family. Thank you Colin Kaepernick for taking a stand for equality. Thank you, *Black Lives Matter* for your consistency in making a difference.

Thank you Ryan Coogler for directing *Fruitvale Station* and showcasing the human condition that we all can improve when it comes to equality. Thank you Sharon Hogg for being my acting coach and introducing me to the amazing Laval Belle. Laval, thank you for your words of wisdom. Mom, I can't thank you enough because of what you have sacrificed for me is beyond words and it is priceless. I want to thank everyone who took the time to read this book and supported me on this journey. I want to leave this with you. It's a quote that I feel GOD gave me, "If you die today would you get an A plus on life's report card? If not and you are blessed to see tomorrow, live like it's extra credit because tomorrow's not promised. We are all six degrees of separation from making a different choice and loving each other."

Table of Contents

Carlos Martin

Introduction

One reason it took so long to write *A War on Friendly Grounds* is because of fear and PTSD. Honestly, I was hurt, depressed, and had anxiety. I received all types of calls, thank you's, offers to riot, and death threats after my interview with Roxy, Hot 97 and CNN. I didn't believe people wanted to hear what I had to say.

Everything changed for me when I watched *Fruitvale Station* directed by Ryan Coolger, and when Colin Kaepernick took a knee to protest injustice during the national anthem. Colin Kaepernick was willing to put his job and life on the line by sitting during the national anthem. He didn't stop there; he created a solution for the problem with the *Know Your Rights Camp*, which is so inspiring and amazing.

There is a war on friendly grounds in America and we are all losing the battle. How can we call ourselves the United States and there is no equality and so much division? Minorities are being wrongfully killed and it is being caught on camera, yet we do nothing? How did we become so desensitized that it's the new normal? Why do we only care when it affects us personally, but when it affects us as a country, we look the other way? I asked God, why am I still alive when so many others have lost their lives in similar situations? GOD rest their souls. The purpose of this book is to share my story — to speak for the voiceless and build a bridge between the public and the police. You can't see the rainbow without going through the storm!

Chapter 1

Who Am I?

I was born in Benton Harbor, Michigan. It was a beautiful day, my mom recalls. She was at Ms. Jones' house, pregnant and craving peach cobbler. My mom was dating Mrs. Jones' son, Willie, at the time. She already had my older brother Marquese and my sister Trust, and now she was pregnant with me. My mother went back home to my aunt Louise's house. The sun was out as she waddled back to the house. She felt the urge to go to the bathroom and that is when her water broke. She yelled for help and my aunt T.T. came rushing to the bathroom. My mom told her that her water broke and she needed to get to the hospital as soon as possible.

My mom was really nervous on the drive to the hospital because she didn't know if she was going to make it in time. My aunt T.T. was speeding as she drove from Benton Harbor to Saint Joseph's Memorial Hospital in Saint Joseph, Michigan. When they arrived at the hospital my mom was anxious and worried because she had no control over me coming into the world. So, she braced herself on the floor in the back seat of a Monte Carlo and brought me into the world. By the time the nursing staff arrived I had already been born. On my birth certificate it says, "hospital parking lot."

I was named after my amazing uncle, Carl Shannon. I figured that, since my mom had me in a car (a Monte Carlo) and my uncle's name was Carl, she came up with the name Carlos. My uncle used to get on my mother's nerves by cracking jokes all the time. He wasn't there when I was born because he was serving his country in the United States Marines. I was the busy baby of the family. I was always getting into things because I was so active. I wasn't a crier, but I did love to be in the spotlight and enjoyed attention. My brother Marquese, sister Trust and I were all born three years apart.

While in the Marine Corps, uncle Carl was gone for almost a whole year before he came home in 1979 to visit his mother, who was my aunt Louise. When he got there, he went upstairs to the living room and saw a baby crawling around. He asked his sister, "Shirley, whose baby is this?" Shirley is my mom, who is really uncle Carl's cousin. My mom lost her mom when she was 11 years old and she was raised by my aunt Louise. They were all raised like siblings despite the fact they were cousins. My mom did not say anything at first. He asked his mom whose baby was it. No one said anything. He picked me up and looked at me. He put me back down and looked at my mom and said, "Somebody is going to tell me something." My uncle was upset because my mom promised she wouldn't have any more children. She already had two and a promising future to be a teacher at Western Michigan University. My mom took my uncle to the side and asked him if he was upset. He was very upset because she promised not to have any more children. My uncle didn't even know I was named after him until he went back to his duty station. Despite being honored that I was named after him, my uncle was still upset because he wanted the best for my mother.

When I was two years old, my mom gave up on her dream to be a math teacher at Western Michigan and decided to join the United States Army. Marquese and Trust lived with my grandma. My grandma didn't believe mom was really joining the Army. She told my mother to take me with her to California. If she joined the Army, Denise and George, who lived in San Diego, would bring me back to Benton Harbor. So, we drove from Michigan to San Diego, California and lived with our cousin until my mother joined the United States Army. After my mom left for basic training, the Taylors brought me back to Benton Harbor and I lived with my aunt Louise. I was so excited to see my brother and sister again, who stayed in Michigan with my grandma.

About a month after I got back, I went outside to play with my friend David. David and I used to play and share toys all the time. He had a big wheel and I wanted to ride it. He let me ride it and his mom got upset. She put David's big wheel up and told me to get out of her yard. I left and stood by the fence talking to David. My aunt Louise happened to come to the door because she always kept a close eye on me. She saw me crying because I couldn't play with David or ride his big wheel. It broke her heart. So, the next day she bought me the biggest big wheel in the neighborhood. I was so excited to ride my big wheel. They could hardly get me dressed or get me to eat breakfast before I was outside riding my big wheel.

On my first day of school I went to Hull Elementary in Benton Harbor. During this time, my mom received orders to be stationed in Germany. We continued staying at my aunt Louise's house. My aunt Louise raised us in church and we attended Progressive Baptist Church with Rev. Charles. She instilled in us to respect our elders and anyone in position of authority. She made sure we understood that GOD was in control and to trust Him no matter the situation.

One day after school, we came home and Marquese called my aunt Louise "grandma." She ignored him because she didn't know Marquese was talking to her. We always called her aunt Louise. Marquese got upset because she wasn't responding to him. So, he tugged at her gown and said, "Grandma, I know you hear me." That's when it hit her that Marquese called her "Grandma." She smiled and gave him a kiss. We have been calling my aunt Louise "Grandma" ever since.

I was a busy body as a kid and encountered all types of life-threatening situations. One time, I don't know exactly what I was doing but I stuck a button in my nose and couldn't get it out. I went crying to my grandmother. I told her I had button in my nose. She tried and couldn't get it out either. She took me to the hospital and had it removed. I was fine, but the situation scared my family.

There was another time when my papa Glen left a hanger on the table. A book was sitting on top of the hanger and the hook was hanging out over the table. My brother and I were playing tag in the house and he was chasing me around the table. As I ran around the table, I ran into the hook on the hanger and it got caught my right eye lid. I screamed and panicked because of how gruesome it looked.

They took me to the hospital again to get the hanger removed.

I remember another time playing with my cousins Keisha and Zakiyah downstairs and they wanted me to change the channel on the TV. Despite the TV being out of my reach, I stacked some books and reached up to change the channel. When I shifted my weight, the books moved. While I was still holding onto the TV, it fell down on me and busted me in my head. Once again, they took me to the hospital to get stitches. There was another time when Keisha and I took Zakiyah's Smurf-mobile, which is a big wheel. Zakiyah got upset and chased me around and beat me with a stick.

It was a challenge for my mom to be stationed in Germany and have to leave us behind. She loved us, but she made the sacrifice to go to Germany without us to create a better life for us. She looked at it as an adventure. Living in Benton Harbor and working at Whirlpool was not going to provide the lifestyle she wanted for us.

After my mother finally got everything situated in Kitzingen, Germany she called my grandma and told her it was time for us to come to Germany. So, the day we were leaving, my brother and sister got dressed and my grandma dressed me in all white to go to the airport. My grandma drove us to the Chicago airport with my aunt Beverly. We had spent the night at Aunt Beverly's house. We went to the airport in the morning and my grandma put us on the plane. We didn't want to go because we had so much fun with our grandma.

My grandma was so nervous she made the stewardess promise to keep an eye on us and call when we landed. She made sure and gave her phone number to the stewardess. They practically forced my grandma off the plane because my nose started bleeding while we were boarding the plane. My grandmother started crying and they assured her everything was going to be okay. So, my grandmother left. We sat in first class. The flight attendant kept her promise and kept an eye on us. When my grandma got back to my aunt Beverly's house, she took a shot of Hennessy and went to sleep waiting for us to land. When we landed, the flight attendant called my grandmother. My mother met us at the airport in Germany. She called my grandmother to let her know we were safe and that she appreciated everything she had done for her.

Who Am I

Chapter 2

Growing Up Military

When we arrived to Germany I fell in love with sports. It shielded me from all of the things that were missing in my life. When you are an Army brat, you move around a lot. You don't have the chance to make lifelong friends to grow up with because you are always moving. When I played sports, I didn't need any of that because it didn't matter to me. The only thing that mattered was coming together to conquer the challenge in front of us.

I was proud of everyone on my team despite challenges we faced because we would face them together. We didn't win every game, but when we faced adversity it was my job to pick everyone up so we could focus and have fun. There's something magical about focusing on a goal and enjoying it while you do. It taught me that a simple compliment can change a person's perspective. That's why I was the captain of almost every team I played on.

I never knew my father Willie, but I knew that he claimed my sister. It bothered me as a kid to see everyone else's family and I didn't know my family. So, I created my own family through sports. After a while not knowing my father didn't bother me anymore because you can't miss what you don't have. This didn't take away from the love I received at home, but It was something different. My mom had multiple jobs working in the Army and going to school.

I won trophies in every sport I played. The crazy thing about winning is you get so much praise. My coaches became role models and I looked to them as father figures and everyone on my team were my brothers. So, I looked forward to playing sports. My mom had to work a lot. Sometimes she would work extra hours. My brother and sister and I became close. We started bonding through sharing gummy bears and playing games at the DYA, Department of Youth Association. Keece (Marquese) and I started break dancing on cardboard. My brother's crew was so good they used to travel and battle other crews in Germany. My sister was captain of the cheerleading squad and my mom was her coach for the DYA. My mom was also a track star in Germany. I used to collect old trophies from the DYA of former champions. I would imagine what it was like when they won a championship. I always told myself that I would be a champion and be the first professional athlete in my family to play basketball, football, baseball and go to the Olympics. I won my first championship in 1985 playing football in Kitzingen, Germany.

Ft. Lewis, Washington

We lived in Germany for four years. Then my mom received orders for Ft. Lewis, Washington. We lived in Lacey, Washington while we waited for post housing (housing on a military base) at Ft. Lewis. My mother met Rev. Morris at South Bay Elementary School during registration, and he invited us to New Life Baptist Church. So, we drove to Olympia, Washington for church and my mom enjoyed the preaching, choir and most importantly the Youth Program. My mom made all of us join the choir and youth program. I became friends with Wendell Morris Jr., Corey, Ricky Reed, Ander Snipers and George Anthony.

I became especially good friends with George Anthony. I met him at the park while playing basketball with the other kids from New Life Baptist Church. George had a nice jumper. So, I picked him to be on my team and we ran the basketball court at the park. When we were done playing we went back to the church and found out that our parents became friends as well. It's funny how GOD worked and allowed us to become friends. His mother was Sarah Wilson, his sister Victoria, brother Frank and his aunt Sharon. They all lived in Lacey, Washington while we lived on the Army base in Ft. Lewis.

One day while visiting George and his family, George and I went outside to play. We rode our bikes out of the neighborhood to play basketball. Aunt Sharon told her husband, Uncle K, that we left the neighborhood. Uncle K asked me why we left and I told him because George and I wanted to play basketball. We left the park and went to our homes. I got a call later from George saying he got a butt-whipping for going to the park. George said he took one for the team. We went to their home every Sunday after church for dinner. Uncle K was like a father figure to us despite having his own children Tony, K.K., and Christina.

George claims I was the square one out of both of us, but I was just smart and kept him out of trouble. If any situation came up, I would talk George out of fighting. When Christmas came around, we called each other bragging about getting a Nintendo and the Nintendo power pad. I was really good at video games and taught George how to use his hands instead of his feet to make the players run faster. I showed him how to turtle tip on Super Mario Bros to get extra lives and the Super Contra code. We were like brothers. We were probably closer than I was to my older brother because we were the same age.

I went to Hillside Elementary School, which is on Ft. Lewis. My sister went to Woodbrook Middle School and my brother went to Lakes High School. We didn't have a perfect family and we didn't always see eye to eye. My mom was hard on us because living an Army lifestyle isn't easy. One day, while my mom was disciplining my brother Marquese, he wanted to run away and stay with his friend Mike. So, he packed up his things when my mom wasn't looking and left the house. For some reason my brother thought it would be better to stay with Mike's family. He called himself running away even though Mike only lived three blocks away. When you're a kid you think three blocks is three cities. I ran after my brother in my pajamas screaming and yelling "I love you and I don't want you to leave. I want to go with you and I'm not going to let you go." My brother stopped running because he could see me chasing him and I wasn't going to stop. He was crying and told me he loved me. He told me I couldn't go with him and I need to go back in the house. I chased him again, but when I saw I wasn't going to catch up to him I just cried in the street. When my mom realized we were not in our rooms, Trust told her what happened. My mom immediately got in the car and drove down the street. She told me to get in the car and we went to get Marquese from Mike's house. Marquese came back home and everything went back to normal for a while.

I caught my sister kissing a boy one time and smoking cigarettes. I told my mom and she whipped my sister. She made her eat a pack of cigarettes to teach her a lesson. My sister was so upset with me for telling on her. She said I was mean because I was always telling jokes and I didn't care how it hurt people's feelings. I didn't understand why she was taking it so personally if she knew I was joking.

My mom met a gentleman named Andre in the Army. Before he got arrested, they became really good friends. Andre was arrested for murder because a man was molesting his daughter. He was sentenced to prison for 15 years. They became pen pals and she began visiting Andre in prison. They started a relationship and were were married. Quote from my Mom's book, "What Mommies Need to Know":

"My husband was a former soldier, and we met in the Army. There has always been a wild side of me that was too scared to experience the wildness directly, but I wanted to share a part of it for some crazy reason from a distance.

I answered that voice and married my husband after he had gotten in trouble while in the military. I had a jailhouse wedding. Yep, I did it and I had my family and friends support my decision. Well, most of them supported. All I wanted at that time was to be married to someone whom I thought truly loved me.

Well, I must say it is my belief that my husband really did grow to love me but it wasn't his initial focus. Believe it or not I actually grew to love him as well after we married. What a crazy way to make a choice but doggone it, I did it based on my unskilled or unclear emotions.

Visiting my husband in prison wasn't the greatest thing I imagined for my life. In fact, if someone would have told me this story I would have snarled my nose or cursed. Often times, I asked myself why I did settle for this type of lifestyle. I am unclear and unsure but I think I know why and I will reveal this toward the end of the book.

I just know that I don't regret it totally because my husband was a good man to me when he was functioning without drugs. Now, the monster that he allowed to appear in our lives was another story. Well okay, I had a monster inside of me also but I made every attempt to tame mine. I am not saying he did not attempt to tame his, but I will say that his monster won.

Yes, he went back to drugs, which ultimately led to his death. I won't forget the night he told me that he needed help and I didn't know what to do. I had never used crack so I had no clue on what to do or to expect. Here I go again, I was in denial. I was in denial that this elephant was way too big for me to digest.

There were several lessons I learned from this marriage that has made me a better individual. I realize that in order for me to heal and be set free I must let go of any shame in my life. What I had to realize was that I hadn't done anything to go to prison. Neither did I choose to smoke a substance that took total control of my very being, leaving me with no other recourse but to answer its call when it called my name. I didn't choose to end it all by committing suicide. I am not judging or saying I was better than my husband but I have to admit in most cases I made better choices.

Yes, life sometimes presents us with multiple choices but we are in charge or in control of our choices and decisions. His actions impacted everyone involved in our lives. My husband again had a phenomenal character to be a good husband and father. He was the answer to helping me deal with the molestation. I could talk to him and he understood. Little did I know but he told me that he, too, had been molested as a child. Nonetheless, his little negative voice brought not only danger to him but danger to everyone he loved and who loved him."

During the time they were dating, my mom used to make us go to the prison. I wasn't cool with visiting Andre in prison, but when you're a kid what can you do? I remember driving three hours from Monroe, Washington to the prison. I'll never forget looking at the wall, which looked like they were 50 feet high with barbed wire all around them.

As we entered the visiting room, I remember checking in at the front desk and looking at all of the other families waiting to see their loved ones. Eventually, when it was our turn, we went through the metal detectors, which led to the visiting room. I saw all the inmates sitting at the table with their families. Andre came out from the back wall after being searched. They removed his handcuffs. He said hello and gave my mom a hug. I went to the play area and just played Pac Man the whole time during our visit. I got really good at Pac Man and broke the high score. Andre was a good guy despite being in prison. He wanted to play the role of my father, but he wasn't my father. Eventually, Andre and my mother were married and I was the ring bearer in prison. I didn't want to be, but I knew it would make my mother happy.

After they were married my mom was allowed to have conjugal visits. So, we spent weekends inside the prison. I just stayed in the front and played my video games. Video games became my escape from reality. I would be so focused on the video game I forgot it was a prison. I got in trouble one day at school for talking in class and my mom told Andre. He told me I couldn't go anywhere and tried to act like my father. I told him he couldn't go anywhere and that he wasn't my dad, and I didn't need him to try to act like my dad. I told him I respected him for loving my mom and as a man, but don't try to act like you're my father! My mom was angry with me, but I was hurt that she would try to force him on me. I told her to stop forcing me to go to the prison. That was her life and she shouldn't force that on me. That really messed up my relationship with my mom because she couldn't understand where I was coming from.

Andre and I eventually became cool. We talked about life and the curveballs it throws at you. We talked about the system and how it was important to stay out of trouble. He used himself and his situation as real life lessons on how corrupt the system can be, especially for a black man. He sheltered us from the dark side of being in prison and life. I knew my mom was a hard worker and she gave up her dreams to give us a better life. I just didn't understand why she chose Andre.

The following year I went to Woodbrook Middle School and my mom came down on orders for Korea. It was a good and bad time. My brother moved back with his dad Marcus Hayes. Marcus had two other children,

Marquette and Peaches, and he was married to a woman named Flora. My sister moved back to Michigan with my grandmother and I stayed with aunt Sharon in Lacy. I went to Chinook Middle School in Lacey, Washington with my friend George.

When we went back to church, we were "adopted" by Rev. Mumpherd. George and I were chasing the girls at church. Where they went, we went. I could sing. So, I led songs in the church choir. George was a rapper. So, that's the path he went down. W.D. was the pastor's son and he played the drums. I dressed well because my mom sent me clothes from Korea. I was the cool kid everyone wanted to be around, which worked for me because my family wasn't around. I always played sports and brought fun with me everywhere I went. I was never a bully, but I was always the one protecting everyone. I guess when everything is taken from you, you become protective of everything you can.

George and I were going to a party. Before leaving for the party, I found out George had been in a fight with the girl's brother. It didn't have anything to do with me so I went to the party. I told George he had to go home because he didn't know how to act. He was so upset he told my sister. When I got home from the party she asked me why did I go without George. I told her I'm not going to let him stop me from having fun because he didn't know how to act. George apologized for the situation and understood where I was coming from. Besides, he went downtown and just hung out with this other friends. I always did my best to live right and stand up for what is right. I've been that way my whole life. It's in my DNA.

I missed my family but I thank GOD for making me strong and surrounding me with good people. I always had such amazing men in my life to keep my head on straight. Plus, being active in sports, I was never distracted by gangs or drama. I just wanted to fit in and have friends.

While we were in school, George and I went our separate ways because he was always fighting and gang banging. He ended up in boarding school. So, I would only see him on the weekends. Andre and I started hanging out more while George was going to mental hospitals. George never got in trouble because I wouldn't let him get into trouble. He was a good person. People just misunderstood him and he made some bad choices. So, when we hung out I made sure we were having so much fun he couldn't get into trouble. My mom found out that George was gang banging and fighting. So, she sent me back to Michigan to live with my aunt Iris, who was married to R.C. Gulley. They had two boys Shackey and Sheldon, and one girl Teresa. Sheldon and I looked like twins.

While in Michigan, me, Shackey and Sheldon went to a recreation center called the Loft to watch all the games. We had a clique called the Midget Mob and we used to act out the Five Heartbeats. I was in a marching band and played the saxophone. I was second chair out of all the saxophone players. One time, we were marching in the Blossom Parade and had to cross the St. Joseph Bridge. I was afraid to cross the bridge because I could see the water when we crossed the drain bridge. I freaked out and panicked and the teacher had to help me across the bridge.

Ft. Bragg, North Carolina

My mom received orders for Ft. Bragg, North Carolina. So, my sister Trust went back to Washington to help my mom pack up and move. We traveled from Washington State all the way to North Carolina. Mrs. Joann, from the church, rode with us in the U-Haul truck. It was a long drive and Ms. Joann snored so bad no one could get any sleep. So, I had to sleep during the day, when she was awake, to get some rest. I also put my earphones on when she went to sleep because of the loud snoring.

Along the way, we stopped by one of my mother's friend's house. She was a nice old lady named Gwen. She invited us into her house to spend the night. Marquese met us there in North Carolina because we were all going to Carowinds Amusement Park in the morning. When we were in Ms. Gwen's home, you could tell she was a hoarder because stuff was everywhere. I asked her if I could go in a room and play video games. She was cool with it so I went in the bedroom and played video games. While I was in the room I got this weird feeling, but I didn't want to lose. So, I ignored it. I couldn't shake this feeling so I turned on the light in the room. I saw roaches everywhere! They were all over the wall and on the ceiling! I have never seen so many roaches. I didn't know they were so fast and that they could fly. I ran out the room screaming and my brother asked if I was okay. I told him to walk in the room and to be careful. My brother went into the room and saw the nightmare of roaches. He looked at me and told me to be quiet because he knew I had a big mouth. Ms. Gwen came by and asked what was wrong, but I told her everything was fine knowing I was lying. I didn't want to be rude, but dear GOD! She asked me if I was hungry and if I wanted to eat. I told her no. I definitely didn't want anything to eat from her house even though I was starving. I told my mom I was going to sleep in the U-Haul. I refused to sleep in a house full of roaches. My mom slept in the house. Marquese was sitting in the house and he kept flicking the roaches off him. He got tired of doing that and decided to sleep in the U-Haul with me. I waited until we stopped at a gas station, just before Carowinds, to wash up in the bathroom. Then I got something to eat before going to the amusement park. My brother and I raced all over Carowinds to be first in line for the roller coaster rides. We had an amazing time as a family.

My brother went back to Michigan. We moved into a hotel on Ft. Bragg base while waiting for military housing to open, but there was no post housing. So, they built a neighborhood in Raeford, North Carolina, which we called 801. This is where all the military people stayed if you didn't live on post. We lived about 30 minutes from Ft. Bragg. I went to Hoke County High School my freshman to junior year. It was tough being a freshman at a new school because I had to make new friends. So, I became friends with all the military kids who lived in 801. In my freshman year I played football for our school. We were so bad we only scored one touchdown all season. The one time I had an opportunity to score on a kickoff return my teammate tripped me while he was celebrating at the five-yard line. My favorite teacher was my Spanish teacher, Ms. Wiles.

My mom was big on church. It seemed like we went to church every day of the week. There was a guy named James who came to the youth center and preached to all the kids in the neighborhood. We were all in a circle praying one day and he looked at Eddie and said, "Now you're saved." Eddie ran home crying because he wasn't ready to be saved. He said he had more sinning he wanted to do because he was still a virgin.

We all played basketball at the outdoor courts. Everyone knew my mom was super strict. We were playing basketball one day and I was supposed to be grounded. In the middle of a fast break I made a layup and kept running home like Forrest Gump because my mom had just driven past us going home.

I used to have a basketball court set up in my front yard where everyone in the neighborhood would come play basketball. It was an adjustable basketball goal. We would lower it so we could have dunking contests. We didn't even let the cement dry before we started dunking on the court. So, the basketball goal spun when we dunked.

Everyone played at Brian's house because it was right in front of the bus stop. Tramine was the oldest out of the 801 crew and he boxed. He would have us outside boxing. One time when I was boxing with Tramine, I faked a right cross and hit him with a hook right on the jaw. Tramine smiled and looked like he was about to kill me. So, I took my gloves and ran. We would do stupid things like jump over trash cans. John, who sagged his pants really low, tried to jump over the trash can. He tripped and fell into the trash can and rolled down the hill.

Life was crazy. Everyone thought we were rich because our parents were in the military and the military built a neighborhood in this country just for us. What's crazy is they dressed better than we did and most of them had cars while we took the bus to school. They thought we were so privileged because of the military. One day they came to 801 for a rival basketball game. The game came down to the wire and we played the best of three or five depending on the sunlight. I was there for the first two games, but my mom came home and I had to leave. After I left I heard the game came down to a final shot and Cliff got fouled real hard. A big fight broke out on the basketball court between the teams. A young man from the rival team got knocked out and they had to pick him up and take him home. They went back to their neighborhood and told everyone at school they got jumped by all the military kids in 801.

On the way to school the next day everyone was telling me about the fight. When we arrived, it looked like every student in the school, teachers included, was outside ready to fight us. It was so bad the bus driver had to call the police. When we got off the bus everyone ran and were chasing us. Everyone knew I was on the football team. So, some people gave me a pass. When the police showed up we were sent home from school.

My Senior Year

In my senior year I went to live with my brother Marquese in Michigan. I wanted to go to Everett High School with Q.T. but Marquese lived too far away from his other brother for us to go to school together. So, I went to East Lansing High School because I transferred from another high school. I wasn't allowed to play football. The school didn't want it to look like they were recruiting me, but if the team made the playoffs they would allow me to play. So, I stayed on the team and trained. I went to the University of Cincinnati where there was a huge statue of Oscar Robinson. We did spring training there to show off our talents and skills. We got to play against the college football players to see what the next level was like. I had an amazing time at camp. I got to network and pick a lot of college athletes' brains. When we reached the game before the playoffs, we'd lost to Sexton by a touchdown. So, I didn't get to play football my senior year. I was so hurt because I loved football. I thought it was stupid that I couldn't play because I moved to Michigan from North Carolina. They should have made an exception to the rule for the military kids.

My niece Teasha came to visit my brother and I while we lived in this nice, old house. One day when my brother had a female guest over, my niece was eating a popsicle and dropped it on the stairs. My brother went off on my niece because there were ants all over the place. I told my brother to calm down because Teasha didn't mean to drop the popsicle. Marquese told me to shut up, it was his house and if I didn't like the rules I could get out. This was the first time my brother and I got into a fight. He hit me in the cheek and I punched him in the eye and we started to wrestle. After we were done fighting he called my mom and told her I need to move to Anchorage, Alaska where she was stationed. I was only trying to protect my niece. I spent the night at Marquese's friend's house. Afterward, I got my plane ticket and moved to Alaska.

Living in Alaska

In Alaska, I attended Bartlett High School and saw my friend Eddie and his sister Shante from 801 in North Carolina. It was nice to see familiar faces at a new school all the way in Anchorage. I honestly didn't think there were any black people in Alaska, but I was definitely wrong.

I inquired about playing basketball, but the season had already ended. Because of weather conditions in Alaska sports start early. So, I missed out playing basketball my senior year. I didn't think there was any chance of being recruited to college, especially coming out of Alaska. My P.E. teacher and coach wanted me to repeat my senior year so I could get a football scholarship. My mom was totally against it. I just finished running track and was number four in the states, high jump, long jump and triple jump. We could have won first place in the 4 x 1 relay race but we were disqualified because of a teammate's uniform.

After I graduated from high school, I worked at the airport as a ramper for Alaska Airlines. A ramper is person who takes the passengers' luggage from the plane to the conveyor belt in the terminal. I worked there with Eddie from 801. What's so crazy is we had the same birth date, middle name, and attended the same high schools. I drove us to work and we made $25 an hour, sometimes more during the holiday season. I saw so many families coming and going through the airport. Part of me was jealous that they could travel together as a family. Eddie and I talked about our future and what we wanted out of life. Eddie said he was going to join the Army and I thought about joining with him. I wanted to play football, but I honestly didn't have the grades for a football scholarship. I didn't take the SAT test because I was always moving around. My coach understood my circumstance, but felt I would do better pursuing a career in sports.

Chapter 3

Life as a Soldier

I got caught with a girl in my mom's home, so she said it was time to get out of her house. I never wanted to be a gangster and I couldn't get into the college I wanted. So, I decided to join the military. I took the ASVAB test, passed and joined the Air Force. When the time came for me to do basic training, the recruiter called and said, "Airmen Martin, are you ready to join the Air Force and be a parachute rigger?" I said,"Huh? We talked about me working in personnel. What are you talking about?" He said after three years I can change my job to personnel. I told him I no longer wanted to join the Air Force because he lied to me. So, I enlisted in the Army instead and became a Medical Records Specialist 91G, which is now a 68G.

I joined the Army and my mother was so proud of me because I was following in her footsteps. Honestly, I was using it as a stepping stone for college so I could play football. I went to basic training in Ft. Benning, Georgia, which was the home of the infantry called Sand Hill. My mom had connections in the Army and talked to my drill sergeant without me knowing. Boy, was I in for a surprise when I got there. When you arrive at basic training it's a setup. Everybody's talking all nice and being respectful, meeting other young people who decided to represent their country and put their life on the line. I was a little nervous because I didn't know what to expect. I thought I was being smart because I knew a little about the system from Andre and how things worked. I shaved my head bald before I went to basic training so I wouldn't have to worry about a haircut.

Basic Training

The bus finally came and the drill sergeants politely asked us to get on the cattle bus. We got on the bus and waved goodbye to our family. I had so many mixed emotions as the cattle bus left. As soon as we turned the corner shit hit the fan. The drill sergeants turned into monsters and started cussing everyone out. They talked about your family, girlfriend, and how she was going to have sex with "Jodie" while you were in basic training. They were yelling at the top of their lungs looking to break us. I thought it was funny because I grew up in a sports and military family with people talking trash all the time. But when I looked around I saw people crying and trying to break out of the cattle bus. It was so bad that some soldiers even peed on themselves. It felt like we were on a trip to prison.

When we arrived in front of our barracks the drill sergeants were throwing everyone's bags off the bus. They didn't care whose bag it was, it had to get off the bus, period. They rushed everyone off the cattle bus despite some fighting to stay on. You were definitely going to get off the bus the easy way or the hard way. Remember, this is the home of the infantry and they didn't play that. The drill sergeant told everyone to get into formation for roll call. We all lined up and got into formation and he called us all DICKS!

We all looked around like, "What are you talking about?" So we laughed and made jokes about the drill sergeant's comments. That really set him off even more. He said, "A D.I.C.K. is a Dedicated Infantry Combat Killer." That was a stupid acronym and I shook my head. He caught me shaking my head and said, "I know you because your mom is in the military. You're going to be the company's battle buddy partner." What that meant was if anyone got into trouble, I was in trouble with them. The drill sergeant then yelled out, "Beat your face!" which meant he wanted us to drop down and give him ten push ups. A nervous soldier took it literally and started punching himself in the face. The drill sergeant tackled him and asked, "What the hell is your problem? Do you have mental issues?" He responded, "No. I'm just a D.I.C.K., a Dedicated Infantry Combat Killer, and I will do whatever you say."

The drill sergeant made us find our bags that were near the cattle bus. When we all got our bags, he took us upstairs after smoking us, which meant we had to workout until we almost died before we could go to our barracks. When we got upstairs, we stood around the Kill Zone, which is a big rectangle in the middle of the floor. If we got into trouble we had to work out in the middle of the floor. Then the drill sergeant yelled, "Grenade in the bay!" We looked around at each other because we had no clue what he was talking about. The drill sergeant told us when he says, "Grenade in the bay!" we have to take all of our belongings and throw them out of the window. Then we have to go downstairs, pick them up and put them back nice and neatly into our lockers. Every time we did not pass inspection, he would call grenade in the bay.

No one got any sleep the first night. The next morning at 0500 we had to get dressed for P.T. (physical training). It seemed like we ran forever. We did push ups until we couldn't push anymore. We did sit ups until we threw up because our stomachs were so tight. We did mountain climbers until we got bruises from our knees hitting our chest. It felt like my guardian angel was in the best shape of his life because of how we worked out.

The next day we got haircuts. I thought I was smart by shaving my head bald before going to basic training. So, I told the drill sergeant, "I'm good because I'm already bald and I came to basic training prepared." He said, "Okay, private, you think you smart by shaving your head, but you're going to do the same thing as everyone else." So, despite having a bald head the barber shaved my bald head again as if he was really cutting my hair. I couldn't believe it because he really took his time like I had hair on my head. He started a conversation as if I was back home on the block. My drill sergeant watched and I saw that he was testing me to see how I would respond in a crazy situation, but I kept my cool and stayed focused.

We went to the company to pick up uniforms, boots, dog tags, socks, and T-shirts. We took them back to the barracks where we learned how to make our beds with hospital corners, buff the floors, clean the bathrooms, and fire guard. Fire guard is when one person stays up and watches over everyone while they sleep. It helps prepare you for war because you always have to watch your six, which means rear. When we received mail the drill sergeant would always talk about Jodie, a person who is supposedly sleeping with your girlfriend while you're at basic. Then he would throw the mail in the middle of the kill zone, which we were not allowed to enter without getting smoked. So, we had to pay the price to get our mail. He always talked about the 12-inch box, which is the little square on the tile floor. We had to do push ups inside the box, jumping jacks inside the box, anything he could make up until we could do no more.

There was always one soldier afraid to take showers so he would stink, and the drill sergeant would smoke everyone until the soldier decided to wash. Everyone would be so pissed off that they wanted to throw a blanket party for the soldier. A blanket party is when the soldier gets hazed and thrown into the shower even with his clothes on until he decides to shower. I took up for him and told him just shower. I took a lot of heat for that, but if we were a team we are only as strong as our weakest link. I tried to explain this to the other soldiers that this situation probably happens all the time and that the drill sergeant was testing us to see if we would fall apart as a unit. I told them if we can't handle this situation how could we handle situations like this when people's lives are on the line. I got into trouble with the rest of my fellow soldiers. I understood their frustration, but what doesn't kill you will make you stronger. Other soldiers talked about me because they knew my mom was in the Army. It got frustrating at times and they pranked me, but I knew my day was coming. What they didn't know was I knew pugil stick was coming and it would be a chance for everyone to release their frustration. A pugil stick is a long stick with styrofoam on both ends that we used as weapons in our competitions. So, when we had our battles, I was ready for the big payback.

Most people didn't know how to fight using a pugil stick, but I did. So, it gave me an advantage. Plus, I played sports my whole life and I have always been competitive. I won our company battles with a pugil stick and I was feeling myself. In life, there is always someone bigger and better than you. Eventually, your ego will cause you to lose focus and it only takes one second to be humbled. We went back to back for the finals and I thought I would still be able to use my speed against this country boy from Louisiana. So, I turned around to swing and hit him in the face and it was at that moment I knew I messed up. He ducked and spun and hit me in my leg, knocking me off my feet. After that he beat the brakes off me because

I had the wind knocked out of me when I hit the ground.

My drill sergeant told me, "Pride will cause you to fall the moment you disrespect it. There's a price to pay with success, but a turtle will never move if he doesn't stick his head out." So, I lost and let my team down, but I learned so much from losing. It taught me about myself and how to be present in the moment instead of letting the moment control me and my emotions. We went back to our company and got smoked for losing, but it was also a defining team moment. For the first time we all bonded together as a unit. The power of losing can be incredible if you take the time to find the blessing in your mistakes. Losing forces you to look at yourself and work on your flaws.

We went to the firing range to learn how to shoot an M16 and throw grenades. People swore up and down they knew how to use a weapon and they were not afraid to throw a grenade. Well, there are always three sides to a story -- the truth, your side, and their side. One thing about telling the truth is the story never changes. So, we started firing at the range and most people didn't perform the way they thought they would. Some people passed their own expectations while others were afraid of the recoil of the weapon. When we finished we had to learn how to break down a weapon and clean an M16.

When we marched to lunch we had a unit lunch battle. We had to march in chow formation and sing cadences against other companies and squads. Whoever was the loudest and sang the best cadence got to eat first while the other squad watched. I was the platoon leader and I marched and led cadence to the lunch battle. We had to recite THE LAW!

> *"The law, this is our domain.*
> *Are we not men? No, we are not men.*
> *We are beasts and you have made us beasts.*
> *We will not walk, we will not talk.*
> *We will not gather in the night.*
> *We will only dress right, dress right, dress.*
> *Ready, front! And as the last resort use code*
> *blue shield,*
> *And stab between the second and third rib*
> *and twist.*
> *Arrrrhhhhh! Shadow."*

We won lunch battles and we lost lunch battles. When we lost we had to look through the glass window and watch everyone else eat their food.

Soldiers were not allowed to eat doughnuts without maxing P.T. P.T. is scoring at least 90 on all three tests: push ups, sit ups, and the 2-mile run, each one was worth 100 points would give the soldier taking the test 270 points. I scored a 290 on my P.T., but I got in trouble because, what type of leader eats doughnuts if the rest of his team can't enjoy it with him? A real soldier never leaves his team behind. Leaders understand the hard choices it takes to make everyone greater. I was in the best shape of my life. I was able to run 2 miles in 11 minutes and 30 seconds. I was able to do 100 push ups and 100 sit ups for my P.T. test.

We had to do road marches for 15 miles while carrying our rucksacks, equipment and weapons. There were obstacle course challenges, team and individual obstacle courses. We repelled down walls, low crawled under barbed wire, set tents and ran wires so the tents could have power. We set up a gate guard and created 360 perimeters. We learned CPR and land navigation.

The Gas Chamber!

Nothing could prepare us for the gas chamber! The objective was to show us that the gas mask and suit worked. The lesson was if you are the least essential person on the mission they will take your weapon and tell you to remove your mask first. The military would rather sacrifice one person instead of losing everyone.

So, we put on our suit and mask and we marched because we had to be comfortable moving around. As we were marching through the woods I could see a building in front of us. We knew that life just got real. Soldiers cried, others were ready to run away and some looked forward to the challenge. I was all three. I wanted to run, but I knew if my mom did it I can do it too. The drill sergeant commanded us take off our masks to prove there were no chemicals in the building. We were all safe and we started doing push ups. Then he made us sing the national anthem. When we started singing and got to a big note he yelled out, "GAS, GAS, GAS!" Everyone panicked and started choking and coughing but there was no way out. He got us! Those who could handle the pressure got the mask on and cleared the air. The drill sergeant warned us not run but no one listened to his warning.

Some started choking, snot running down their nose and tears running down their face. At that point, we couldn't see and the drill sergeant opened the door. We all ran out the door and all you could hear was, "Ooooow, ooooooooow, ooooooooww!" The drill sergeant laughed and said, "I told y'all rule number 1 not to run." When we took off our masks we saw what the chemical felt like. We walked out and saw the rest of our group getting off the ground. What they didn't know was there was a big tree right outside the door and they ran into it. The drill sergeant laughed at us for not listening. It taught us an important lesson, if you panic in a high pressure situation it could cost your life.

Ft. Sam Houston

After basic training I went to Ft. Sam Houston for A.I.T. (Advanced Individual Training). This is where I learned to be a 91G, which is now a 68G. That stands for Medical Records Specialist. I learned about medical records and how to file the paperwork that goes inside of the record. We were taught how to do medical coding, hospital bed counts, and Admissions and Dispositions. The records were coded because only men were allowed at Ft. Benning, home of the infantry.

I joined the flag football team and led them to a championship. I won my first Commanders Cup and Army coin. There was a drill sergeant who swore she could predict the future. She told me I would either get into trouble because people didn't understand me or I would do something great with my life because people finally got it. I thought she was crazy acting like Ms. Cleo trying to predict the future.

When you're in A.I.T. you can wear regular clothes. You have to pass all of your tests and prove to the drill sergeant that you are Army ready before returning to civilian life. I passed and moved into the purple phase. It was nice to get my civilian clothing and function as a medical specialist.

Ft. Hood, Texas

I received my first orders to Ft. Hood, Texas, 61st Bravo Company and was transferred to 1st Med Brigade. I maxed out my P.T. test, and became the First Sergeant's (1SG) driver. We went to the motor pool where all of the military vehicles were located. I drove the humvee, deuce and a half, and the LMTV. When we went to the field I drove the First Sergeant to the field. When we put up tents, I helped the officers put up their tents because they didn't know how. The officers put the tents up first then tried to put the camo (camouflage) net over it, which was totally wrong. You have to put the net up first and then the tent. It's too difficult to put the tent up first and try to throw the camo net over it and then raise it off the tent.

While we were in the field I received my first AAM (Army Achievement Medal) as a Private (PVT) and was promoted to Private Second Class (PV2). I learned a quick lesson because I thought I would be working in the hospital. In the Army you are a soldier first and your MOS (Military Occupational Specialty) is second.

My NCO (Non-Commissioned Officer) saw that I was in great shape and asked if I wanted to join special forces. I thought that was amazing and my mom would be proud of me. So, I started training with him. We would hit the gym, run five miles, carry logs on our backs, do squats, pull ups and dips. He had me try out for the Soldier Of The Month competition because it was important to understand the rules and regulations in the Army. I went to Soldier Of The Month board and finished in the top three. We went back to training and he shared with me the different levels we would encounter in special forces. He talked about SERE (Survival Evasion Resistance and Escape) training and how they would drop you off in the woods to test your survival skills. If you got caught they could break up to three inches of bone on your body to see if they could get information from you. When I heard about them breaking up to three inches of bone, that was my last day of training.

The NCO continued training and passed, but I wanted no part of that. I will say training with him helped my P.T. score. I was able to run two miles in 11 minutes and 30 seconds. I ran in the A group, which is the top group, and they are able to run their P.T. in 13 minutes or below. I moved to 1st Med Brigade where I worked in the S-3 and ran reports. I was promoted to a PFC (Private First Class), which is an E-3, and got security clearance because of the reports I was running.

I went out for the flag football team and played wide receiver, safety, kick return, and punt return. We won the post championship and brought the trophy back. I learned two things that day, if you play sports and you're good, it will get you out of work. It makes the commander's resume look good. Second, it's an easier way to get awards and you're promoted faster.

I played every sport they had to offer and it made my life in the military so much easier. The funny thing about success is it brings hate. Others see you moving through the ranks faster. So, when you have someone who outranks you they will do anything to slow your process down. I received counseling statements from my superiors for whatever they could think of or make up. If you stay focused, no matter what anyone says and you keep GOD first, what people use against you can actually turn out to be a blessing in disguise.

We created a flag football team called the Untouchables which were made of the best players in different units and we played in tournaments. I was known by everyone on post for my athletics and I was unaware a recruiter came to watch me play. We won the tournament and he offered me a scholarship to Mississippi State Valley. It was like everything finally fell into alignment because I always wanted to play college football with a chance to go pro. I called my mom out of excitement and told her the news. The only problem is I had just reenlisted and was ordered to go to Germany. I went back to my 1st SG and told him about the offer I received to play college ball. He told me Uncle Sam would not let me out of my contract. I was devastated that I had to go back to the scout and tell him the Army wouldn't let me out of my contract. I had to go to Germany. After I left Ft. Hood, there was a mass shooting where one of the officers took his gun and fired at his soldiers.

Germany

I went to Germany and worked at Landsthul Hospital in the medical records room. By this time I was promoted to Specialist, which is an E-4. Everyone rotated jobs to be able to work in any office if it became necessary. So I learned birth registration and correspondence, which is making copies of medical records and calling St. Louis where the military keeps all medical records to recover for soldiers who may need a copy of their paperwork.

I also joined the unit's football team and played quarterback. We had unit revival games against the 212th Mash. All of this was happening between Operation Iraq Freedom and my friends from the 212th Mash going down range, which is being deployed to war. This was the first time in my military career I had to deal with seeing friends go to war. I was doing everything in my power to go down range with my friends. I volunteered to go to war, but they wouldn't let me. I wasn't in their unit and that's not the way the Army operates.

During this time I was working the call center for a night shift and received a call about death threats on Jessica Lynch's life. We informed our NCO of the call and they followed the rules of engagement and safety protocols. Landsthul was the major hospital where the majority of soldiers went if they were injured at war. I worked the Air Evac unit and helped take care of all injured soldiers coming back from war. I would see friends return with shrap metal in their bodies. I remember a girl who was run over by a tank and lost both legs, and a soldier who was injured from an explosive. We did our best to make sure everyone was comfortable and helped them on their road to recovery until they returned to their duty station.

I was blessed with the opportunity to play semi-pro football in Germany, and played for the Saarbrücken Hurricanes and the Kaiserslautern Cougars. We had to wear an "A" on our helmets and on our shoulder pads. Only two American players were allowed on the field at the same time. I remember scoring my first semi-pro football touchdown. It was a quarterback bootleg. My nickname on the team was *ich bin ein schwanv*. I didn't know what that meant, but I accepted it because I wanted to be one of the guys and fit in. You know the old saying, "When in Rome do as the Romans do." I started screaming my nickname in the end zone saying, "I am *ich bin ein schwanv!*"
Everyone was laughing at me and in that moment I knew I messed up or there was something wrong. The referee looked at me and shook his head and the team we were playing against was like, "What in the world is wrong with this American?" So, I went back to the sideline while my team was laughing at me and asked my coach, "What is a *ich bin ein schwanv?*" He laughed at me. They were calling me a "dick" the whole time and that is what I was yelling in the end zone. That was one of my most embarrassing moments in life.

During that season my friends had just come home from down range and I was having one of my best games with a scout watching me play. I ran a quarterback bootleg and broke to the sideline for about a 20-yard run. I should have run out of bounds, but wanted to make the big play in front of the scouts and my friends. I cut back towards the middle and the defender put his face mask in my knee. Another hit me from up top and I tore my ACL. I felt it pop and tried to walk on it but couldn't. This ended my season and my big break. They drained 42 cc's of fluid. While I was going in and out from the meds I kept asking the doctor if I could play football again.

I had to go to rehab. I experienced pain everyday trying to get strength and flexibility back in my leg. After rehab I was able to play flag football again. I re-injured during practice doing the option drill. This time I took my time to rehab the right way. My knee healed and I was able to play football again. The Army was undefeated. We were so good they set up an Army and Air Force tournament. This made Landsthul history. The Colonel of the Air Force was the husband of the Colonel for the Army. So, it was a nice rival game. We ended up winning the game. I also became Europe's MVP for flag football.

Ft. Jackson, South Carolina

I came down on order to Ft. Jackson, South Carolina and worked at Moncrief Hospital. I was promoted to Sergeant (SGT) and was placed in charge of the Medical Records Room. This was my first time being in charge of soldiers. It was different because I was an NCO. My peers and I could no longer have the same type of conversations because I was in charge. I had to go from being friends to the person writing counseling statements or inspecting their uniforms. Even though we held each other to Army regulations there's a six-degree separation when your friends' lives depend on the choices you make when going to war.

Chapter 4

Military or Not,
You're Still Three-Fifths of a Man

On Monday, Oct 24, 2005 I was at work until 1700 briefing PFC Carlyle for on-call duty. I arrived home somewhere between 1715 and 1720. When I came into the neighborhood I turned down my street and followed a police car toward the location of my home. I then pulled into my parking spot as the police car circled the parking lot. I nodded my head and waved to the police officer in the squad car thinking he was the courtesy officer. I rolled up my windows, got out of my car and started walking towards my door. As I'm walking I hear a screeching sound in the parking lot. Just before I put the key in my door I heard a voice yelling out saying,"Hey you, come here!" I turned around towards the voice. It was an officer.

I walked to the officer and asked, "How may I help you sir?" He responds, "I'm here because of a noise violation in the neighborhood." I said, "Okay, well, I just got off work. So, it couldn't have been me. I don't blast my music because there's an officer who lives above me. I know better than to be blasting my music in the neighborhood.

I have never had a violation since I have been here." Then he said, "Give me your license and registration." I reached for my wallet and pulled out my military I.D. card, my German driver's license, my Alaska paper license and card that validates my Alaska driver's license. The officer yelled at me like a drill sergeant, "What the hell is this shit? This is not a driver's license!"

I responded calmly because I didn't want any trouble. I stated, "DUDE take a look at my license plate. You can see I still have German plates on my car. I just went to the DMV and haven't had a chance to put my South Carolina plates on my car yet." He got upset because I called him DUDE and he replied, "My name is not DUDE. I'm a Richland County officer." I responded, "You called me 'Hey You.'" He said he called me "HEY YOU" because he didn't know my name. I then responded, "Well, I called you DUDE because I don't know your name." Then he told me I violated some law. I told him I didn't do anything wrong and said, "What is the problem?" Like a flash of lightning he BODY SLAMS me to the ground for no reason.

I called my wife to come outside. I kept yelling until she came. Luckily, my upstairs neighbor heard all the commotion. I know this because she was outside. The officer was on top of me pushing my face into the ground and kneeing me in my side. He stopped to see who was coming outside. I was in my military uniform the whole time this happened! I yelled out, "I'm a U.S. soldier protecting my country, and this is the way I get treated! This is so FUCKED UP! I can't believe this bullshit! You don't have the right to just body slam people because you're an officer. My wife has been to Iraq and I have been deployed to Bosnia and this shit is fucking crazy! I can't believe this!" He said I must not be from around here, he is Richland County police and he can get away with anything because he has higher connections. "You ain't nothing but another black statistic, another notch on my belt."

I had been trained by the best to stay calm under pressure and would not let him push my buttons. My mom always told me, "When a person is doing you wrong, don't be like them because then you are no better than them. You turn away wrath with kindness." Even though I was upset I thank GOD for basic training because I was disciplined enough to keep my cool. I told my wife not to worry about what she was seeing and to stay calm, go upstairs and get the officer. My wife did as I asked and ran upstairs, but to my surprise it was the officer's mom who immediately came back with her.

Both of my arms were behind my back as the officer cuffed my right arm. I asked what in the fuck was he doing, I hadn't done anything wrong. The officer took out his pepper spray and began to spray me to shut me up. I covered my face with my right arm which he had cuffed and held on to my BDU (Army uniform) jacket. Then I held my breath like I was trained. The military taught soldiers when being attacked by gas to hold their breath and put on protective masks. I did what I was taught. I protected my eyes and held my breath to protect my throat.

I used my right arm to protect my eyes because he had the spray can so close to my face. He began to yank me by my cuffed right arm. He was yanking my arm so hard he left bruises and welts on my right arm, which is shown in my medical documents. My arm was bruised and swollen so bad that 14 hours later the doctor could still see the bruises and welts. The doctor asked if I was on drugs because I didn't react to the pepper spray the way he thought I should. I didn't say anything because I didn't want the spray to go into my throat.

The officer kept kneeing me in my side and yanking my arm so he could spray the pepper spray in my eye. He finally stopped trying to drown me with pepper spray. I was curious why he finally stopped. I looked up and saw my wife. She was outside with her camera phone taking pictures. In my head I was thinking thank GOD she got her phone. He must have been startled to see my wife taking his picture. He got on the radio and started calling for help. He yelled, "I need a TASER GUN!" and kept yelling "Help! I need back up!" My wife dashed into the house and I screamed, "BABY, where are you going?"

About five minutes later you would have thought they found OSAMA BIN LADEN. There were six cop cars that came out of nowhere. I put my other hand behind my back after he stopped pepper spraying me. He cuffed both my arms. I said, "All you had to do was stop spraying me because I was already doing what you asked me to do." Next I see all these white cops over me ready to kick my ass. He's still yelling for the taser.

At the same time he was yelling for a taser my wife came back outside. I wondered what in the hell she was doing. She cried out, "What are y'all doing to my husband?" I saw she still had the phone out taking pictures of the situation. Deputy Fields yells out, "Get her black ass, she has pictures of me." Officer Clarke, a 230-pound man, runs to my wife, throws her up against a car in the parking lot and puts her in a full nelson. My wife dropped her cell phone. He handcuffed her, picked her up by her arms and slammed her to the ground face first. My neighbor Sherri Lewis and her son were watching the situation, They ran out and she screamed, "Oh God, what are you doing to them?" Another officer yells out, "If you don't get your black ass back then I'm going to take you to jail too!"

Three different officers frisked my wife after she was detained. They didn't frisk her with the back of their hands but with the front as if they were feeling her up. I couldn't believe it. I felt like I was in the movie *Crash!* Unable to help, unable to do anything for my wife. I was horrified! How could they do this to her? I couldn't do anything but sit there and watch them. At that moment, all I could do was pray and trust in GOD. I yelled out to her GOD is going to take care of us and not to worry. I kept repeating that GOD is going to work everything out!

They put us in separate police cars. They called EMS because Officer Fields used a whole can of mace on me! I told EMS that I didn't want them to touch me or my wife. Finally, the neighbor came home (a Black officer). They wouldn't let us speak to her. I asked if I could have my wife's camera phone because I knew she took at least 10 pictures. (INTERESTINGLY NONE OF THE POLICE CAR CAMERAS WERE ON, AND NONE OF THE VOICE RECORDINGS WERE WORKING IN ANY OF THE SIX POLICE CARS)

I thought when police reports to a situation like this, they turn on the cameras and voice recordings for everyone's protection! Another officer told me that we would have to delete all of the pictures for us to get the phone back. I told him we were not going to delete the pictures. So, he kept my phone. They took my wife's phone illegally and deleted pictures from it. Now we only have two pictures from the incident.

I'm not saying ALL police officers are bad, but this was a damn shame! I was so helpless, but knew there were angels protecting us. I cried out to my QUEEN and asked if she was okay. I told her to stay calm, GOD would work it out. She responded, "This is wrong!" I told her again to calm down and that GOD was going to work it out! My wife cried out, "Somebody please take pictures, get a video camera, or get the courtesy officer!"

By the time they placed both of us in two different police cars, our neighbor, Officer Goins, and the courtesy officer finally arrived. There was another black officer I didn't know. EMS came to the squad car to give me medical attention. I denied medical service because I wanted a documented full body examination on post. The male EMS officer looked into my eyes and said it doesn't look like you have been pepper sprayed because your eyes are not red. I said, "I know because I covered my eyes." He said, "I don't blame you, nobody wants to be pepper sprayed." They were very nice and respected my decision to deny medical care. They proceeded to my wife but I don't know what happened over there because I couldn't see or hear what was going on.

I asked one of the officers to please get the Captain who was the neighborhood courtesy officer. He did and I thanked him. Before the officer arrived, I heard Officer Fields outside the car talking about how he kicked my ass to the other cops. He stated, "I'm glad that Johnnie Cochran is dead! I'm going make sure I take his career away!" I looked out the window and smiled and said, "GOD BLESS YOU!" He began to laugh at me and tell the other officers what I said. I asked Officer Clarke about my wife's phone, if l could see it to make sure there were no nude pictures of my wife. He said he would let me see the phone, but I had to erase all of the pictures. I responded, "HELL NO! That is okay, you can keep them!"

After everything calmed down I saw a couple of officers walk all the way across the parking lot. I assumed they were asking this man questions about what happened. I was wondering why they didn't ask the women who were directly in front of the scene. After most of the officers left I saw about three to four officers in front of the police car talking about the situation. It seemed they were trying to get their stories straight. They made gestures at my wife and laughed for about 45 minutes.

We left the scene and pulled up to the front gate where we waited on the paddy wagon. I was in the car with Officer Fields and he was trying to push my buttons by making comments like how he was going to ruin me and my wife's career. I told him he couldn't take anything that GOD gave me I don't care who he is or what connections he has. The officer next to him asked, "Did you finally move up from a toaster to a microwave?" whatever that meant. I said, "It's funny how you can come out here for a noise violation and it turns into all of this." It's funny what people perceive to be disrespect. But I wasn't disrespectful to him at all and this is how I got treated.

The paddy wagon finally arrived and I got in first. I saw a young gentlemen already sitting down. I felt like a slave sitting in that paddy wagon! It was the second worst feeling ever. The worst was seeing my wife get CUFFED and SLAMMED to the ground. As my wife approached the paddy wagon to get in I heard a police officer say, "So, we're going to the hotel!" Then I heard someone say, "I know you're smarter than this, what is wrong with you?" but it wasn't Officer Fields' voice. I heard Officer Fields say he's glad Johnnie Cochran is dead and we're going to take you to Motel 6. I mean that was so disrespectful to say to a woman especially to a married woman. When my wife got in the paddy wagon she was searched a second time by a male officer. Again, I didn't understand why they didn't get Officer Goins to search her.

We picked all these other people up before arriving at the police station. My wife asked about an officer's name that started with an F. The paddy wagon driver was cool and told her the officer's name was Fields. I said to my wife, "That was the officer who started all of this!" We asked the driver of the paddy wagon questions about my wife's phone and how they took it illegally. After that we joked and talked about football and how he couldn't play anymore because he had a plate in his head at the age of 15Again Officer Fields made the comment about how he's glad Johnnie Cochran is dead! This time the officer who was driving the paddy wagon overheard him and told us he would write a statement regarding those comments. The officer in the paddy wagon heard the disrespectful comment they made to Tashiana and wrote a statement that I'm so grateful for to this day!

My Ex-Wife's Account of What Happened:

"On the day of October 24, 2005 at around the time of 5 p.m., there was a pounding at my door. When I opened the door, it was one of my neighbors upstairs and a couple of children from the neighborhood. They yelled, 'Come out here, they're doing something to your husband.'

I then ran outside to the lot, looked to my left and saw that my husband was being restrained by a Richland County officer. As I walked up, the officer was kneeing my husband in the side in a kicking motion and smashing his face into the concrete with his knee. I was shaking and asking 'What's going on, what did he do?' My husband then said, 'Baby, I'm fine. Stay calm and run upstairs and get the neighbor.'

My neighbor is a Richland County officer. I started towards the stairs, when realizing that her mother, who was also the neighbor who knocked on my door, was standing on the balcony facing the lot. I asked her, 'Is your daughter at home?' She then said, 'No, she hasn't made it here yet.' I then run into my home to grab my camera phone. I came back out, stood in front of the police officer and my husband, and started taking pictures. I took pictures showing how the officer had my husband and that my husband was not resisting. After one of the shots I took, the officer grabbed his mace and started to spray my husband.

I then yelled, 'He's not even resisting, what are you doing?' He then points the spray in my direction and says, 'Get back or I'll spray you, too.' The officer then gets on the radio hysterically asking for help and for someone to bring a taser gun.

I knew exactly why he was sounding like that and knew that something more was about to go down. My instincts told me to retrieve my video camera because my camera would not catch the events as fast as they were taking place. I then ran into the house to try and retrieve my video camera before anymore officers arrived. I searched, but was unsuccessful, in retrieving the battery to my camera. I then decided to hurry back outside.

Upon getting back outside, there were at least eight, if not more, white officers all around my husband. I then stopped, at a distance, and yelled, 'What are you all doing to my husband?' I heard someone say, 'Get her ass, too.' Next thing you know, I have three officers attacking me, slamming me up against a car, and roughhousing me as if I were a man. They then handcuffed me. After that, one of them picks me up and body slams me onto the ground, allowing my face to hit the concrete. Another one of my neighbors who was witnessing the events and holding my puppy yelled, 'Hey, what are you doing to her?' One of the officers on me ran towards her and pushed her, telling her to 'Get back or they'll take her ass to jail, too.' She complied.

While I'm on the ground there are two officers atop of me with their knees in my back. One of them searches me. While I'm on the ground I'm yelling at the top of my lungs, 'Please, if anyone has a video camera or even just a regular camera, please take pictures of this or video tape it.' I also asked for someone to get our courtesy officer who is a Richland County captain.

I'm then asking the officers, 'Are you all's cameras catching this?' They were telling me that yes they were on and yes they got everything. I didn't believe that it was true because not one officer's car, from what I remember, was facing in the direction of the incident. They then read me my rights. My husband is then trying to tell me not to say anything and just stay calm; everything would be okay; we had done nothing wrong. I'm still yelling saying, 'This is wrong, this is some bullshit, you all are so full of shit, I can't believe this.'

Someone then says that they were tired of hearing me talk and instructed for someone to put me in the squad car. They did so. After a while of being in the car, officer Gore gets in and asks if I had any I.D. on me. I say, no. He then asks for my name and the state of my drivers license. I believe he couldn't find my information so he asked for the exact reading of my name on my drivers license. I gave it to him. I asked the officer a series of questions while in the car. I asked what I was being charged with because no one had given me this information yet. I asked how well do the police videos record and do they pick up sound.

I also remember an EMS worker coming up to the car to speak to officer Gore. He had made the remark, 'I should've known it was F__'s ass that had something to do with this.' The officer gave a quick motion for him to be quiet. When he did this I quickly noted his name, which was Matt Young, and after he left I asked the officer his name and this is when I found out officer Gore's name. All I could make out was the 'f' and 'l' sound of the name that the EMS worker said. I was curious about who he was talking about but most importantly the name of the officer who initially harassed my husband.

During this time, officer Goins, my neighbor, had made it home and the captain who is our courtesy officer had also made it to the scene. While in the car I asked where my phone was because it was dropped when the officers violently attacked me. During this time I also lost my shoes. We sat there for a good two hours maybe, and during this time I am asking if my personal effects were secured and if I could get my shoes because it was cold. I never got my shoes. An officer walked up and told me that I could not get my phone because it was going to be held as evidence.

The officer who arrested my husband came up to me and asked for my information once again. I really had nothing to say to him because I was furious at what he had done. So I asked him, 'Is this covered under my rights; do I have to give you my information?' He then said, 'Well, if you don't we will take you down as Jane Doe and you can also be charged with giving false information.' I then said, 'How can you say I gave you false information if I don't give you any information at all? Is this covered under my right yes or no?' He then answered, 'No!' I then gave him my information once again.

He also informed me that my phone was being taken as evidence. He said, 'You sure took some nice pictures of me too. But it ain't gonna help you.' I said, 'Yes it will. It will show that my husband was being orderly and you maced him when he was already cooperating with you.' I asked, 'Well how long will it take before I can get my phone back?' He then said, 'You will get it back at your court hearing but it will be a long time before your court date. You can delete the pictures off the phone and get it back right now if you want.' I then said, 'Oh no, If that is the case then you can keep it.'

While in the car I asked to speak to officer Goins. But they wouldn't unlock the door for her to talk to me. I also called for the captain who was the courtesy officer of our community. He asked if was okay. I stated no but asked him if he could please talk to the witnesses who stood only a few feet from where the incident occurred. He and one other officer took a statement from anyone in the immediate area, but obtained a statement from a young man who was watching from the far end of the adjacent apartment. I later found out that they only got the statement because the man asked them to take one.

After sitting for a while a male police officer opens the door to exchange handcuffs and once again searches me even though a female officer is present.

After a while I was then moved to another vehicle. We then pull off to the front of the apartment gates where we waited until the paddy wagon arrived. While being put into the paddy wagon the officer says I know that you're smarter than this and I replied you're right and that is because I never violated anyone or did anything.

Before I get into the paddy wagon I was searched again by another male officer. While I'm getting searched, Officer Fields is making racial remarks trying to get a reaction out of me such as, 'I'm sure glad that Johnnie Cochran is dead!' I didn't give him the satisfaction of getting me mad so he then makes the comment that we're going to take you to the Motel 6 which I perceived to be a sexual comment! They put me into the truck and we go around the city." (End of Ex-Wife's Account)

Officer Fields' Viewpoint:

Dep. Smith both in the same vehicle as they approached Mr. Martin still did not comply and Dep. Clarke pushed his head down and Dep. Smith grabbed his left arm and got it back behind his back cuffing him up. Then out of nowhere came Mrs. Martin yelling and cursing "what the fuck are you all doing to him fuck you mother fuckers" and she was swinging at me and Dep. Clarke. I told Mrs. Martin at that time you are now under arrest for Breach of Peace and Dep. Clarke stated "67" at that time I tried to contain her but she kicked and hit me several times before I could restrain her Dep. Clarke also tried to get the cell phone in her hand out of it that I had not even taken notice of. I put Mrs. Martin on the ground and handcuffed her up as well. I that point in time Clarke got on the radio and advised central we were 67 two times. Clarke then stated to put Mr. Martin in my car and Mrs. Martin in Gores car who had just shown up. Several units did show up, but it was after subjects were handcuffed and detained. After that we started the paperwork and Capt. Pearson and Capt. Scott both asked me what happen, and I told them. Capt. Pearson as well as Cpl. Austin advised me that he is a regular. While doing the paperwork Mr. martin asked me to loosen his handcuffs and I did for him twice. Mr. martin kept having mood swings while in my car, one min. he was talking normal to me the next he was saying I can't believe they let you be a cop. EMS did respond but both refused medical treatment. The only people that had cuts were Clarke and myself as a direct result for the confrontation. Either subject had a scratch on them as a direct result of my training and using as little force as possible. Mr. martin continued to run his mouth while in my patrol car and laugh saying God was with him. I asked Mr. Martin if he thought it was funny that he ended his career today as a direct result of what took place" he stated God will take care of me. Cpl. Austin advised me to put the phone into evidence because of the pictures taken with it that do show myself in a struggle with Mr. Martin. Mrs. Martin who I talked to for a brief moment ask me about the phone and if she could have it, I told her it was going into evidence and that she could get it when this whole thing is over. She was concerned about other pictures on the phone as was Mr. Martin as I found out later and I told her she could erase all the pictures and have the phone or none of them, she stated keep the phone. I did turn the phone in as evidence.

I had very little contact with Mr. Martin after the incident until he was switched over to the paddy wagon and started saying he has a good lawyer and he is not worried about anything and he will get off of the charges. I did reply your gonna to need a good lawyer because your career is pretty much over. Let it be known that either subject had any injuries (not one cut or bruise on them) and I had little contact with Mr. Martin after the incident occurred. Dep. Clarke continued to tell me just stay away from him well take care of him you do the paper work. The situation was handled as professional as possible and because of my training and patients the only people injured was Dep. Clarke and myself and that was because of the concrete that we cut are hands on. I must say I would not have done anything differently in the situation and I had supervisors confirm that while on scene there.

Officer Clarke's Viewpoint:

Officer Statement:

Master Deputy, J. Clarke On the 24th of October I and Dep. C. Smith responded to an "officer needs assistance caIr~ at Quail Run apartments. Dep. Smith is in ITO status and I am his acting training officer. We were close to the location of the call~ at Percival and Decker blvd and were the closest unit to respond. The last transmission that we received was from Dep. B. Fields who stated clearly over the radio, "10-83 in progress~ SEND ME ANOTHER UNIT"! This was followed immediately be the muffled sound of a struggle. I activated my blue lights and siren and executed a u-turn to respond quickly to the scene. I was not aware as to what was taking place at the Scene, however I was aware that Field's had been dispatched to the location. We were at the entrance of the complex in less than a minute and with siren and blue lights still activated entered the complex. We were unable to locate Fields and asked dispatch for clarification of his position. They,(dispatch) had him "out" at the complex but were unsure of his exact location. Through trial and error and continued calling of Field's I could not locate. Each exchange by field's revealed that he was still in contact with the subject. I could hear stress in his voice and the sound one makes when someone is straining against weight or a greater force. This of course only increased my anxiety level and coupled with the fact that we were unable to find Fields I called dispatch to tell them, "unable to locate"! Other units were getting closer to the' scene and began to assist me in directions and possible locations.

After what seemed like an eternity, we spotted Field's patrol vehicle. We could see Fields lying on top of an unknown black male who was dressed in Army BDU's. Fields was lying across him and was trying to keep him on the ground one could see redness on field's face and that both he and the subject (Martin) were locked in a struggle. I noticed that a crowd was in a semi-circle fashion around both, and they were getting closer. I and Smith exited the vehicle quickly and ran to Fields' assistance. I noticed that Martin was keeping his an arm under him, near his chin area. Fields had a handcuff on the other arm and was having difficulty getting the free arm behind the back of the subject. I heard fields at least twice tell the subject to put bis arm back, the subject would not comply. The subject was cursing loudly and trying to "Leg sweep" fields off him. I grabbed the free arm by the wrist and placed my free hand onto the subjects head. I did this to prevent the cursing and screaming Martin from spitting or biting. In the past I have had both things happen, when dealing with a fighting subject. Most of the crowd had backed up and were standing in the grassy area in front of the apartments. However two female subjects one who would later be identified as Mrs. Martin and another black female~ who was carrying a small,white in color dog, were advancing on us. They were shouting instructions to Mr. Martin, things like "Don't worry baby I'm taking pictures".

I specifically heard Mrs. Martin say "Don't fuck him up"! She ill particular did not like me placing my hand onto the back of Mr. Martin's head. These two females continued to lUDS~ toward us; I felt they were doing this tor two reasons, one to intimidate: the other to take more photos. I yelled several times for all to BACK UP! They continued to get closer. I concentrated on finishing the handcuffing of the male, when Mrs. Martin tried to kick me. Fields to his credit responded to the movement and quickly grabbed her by the hands and pushed her back towards a parked car. I yelled at Fields.

"67"! That way he knew. If there was any doubt, that she (Mrs. Martin) was going to be arrested. This bought me enough time with the assistance of Dep. Smith to complete handcuffing of the male. Martin continued to yell and cuss but suddenly turned his focus on his wife, telling her to calm down. This had absolutely no effect. I moved toward fields that had his hands full of; cursing, screaming, swinging and kicking Mrs. Martin. Fields was lying to bring her under control without injuring himself or the subject.

As I moved towards them the unknown black female with the dog got between myself and Fields. I pushed her back and yelled at her that if she continued to interfere I would place her under arrest. She responded with something like, "Oh my god" and moved backwards. The assembled crowd some of whom were friends of the subjects continued to jeer and taunt us. Realizing how volatile this situation was becoming. I admonished the crowd that any other person that advanced on us would face 8lTest. This seemed to work: and the crowd stayed in place for a moment. I then noticed that Mrs. Martin had a cell phone in her hand and was swinging it at fields.

Due to fields' size and strength he was trying to just "wrap up" Mrs. Martin imd not hurt her. I attempted a "straight ann bar take down)' in the hopes that Mrs. Martin would both drop the phone and lay on the ground; this would not work due to her continued thrashing. I seized the arm which held the cell phone and using a minimal amount of force was able to remove the phone. I informed Martin that she too was under arrest and to stop resisting. She continued to scream in a hysterical fashion and her husband continued to plead with her to calm down, She kept yelling, "I hope someone is videotaping this"

Once the phone was removed from her band, we placed her on the ground and completed handcuffing. 'There was little if any inter-communication between the deputies present, it was mostly a reaction to what we were facing. In fact, I believe I was the most vocal of any, especially in addressing the crowd. Once the subjects had been cuffed I instrUcted that Mrs. Martin be placed in recently arrived deputy Gore's patrol vehicle.

I personally escorted Mrs. Martin to the car and she continued to hurl insults at all present. I reminded her that she had the right to remain silent and "Perhaps she should do that". After hearing her threats of a lawsuit and her taunts, I told her to "SHUT UP"! I sat her in the vehicle and slammed the door. Mr. Martin continued to state how this "was in Gods hands now" and that 'we would all be sorry.' I instructed that Mr. Martin should be placed into

Field's patrol car. To his credit Mr. Martin remained somewhat calm, but his wife turned her venom on all of us. She stated she was going to sue IIS and that we would be sorry. She specifically mentioned that she had pictures, of "police brutality" on her cell phone. Once the subjects were in the vehicles we took stock of the situation and a much needed breather. I noticed that Mr. Martin's army beret with tom off insignia was lying on the ground. This just hammered home the amount of struggle, I also noticed Mrs. Martin's cell phone on the ground. All items were collected and placed onto the trunk area of a patrol cat. I confirmed with dispatch that we were 67,(2) times and that an ambulance was enroute. We had EMS respond per policy, due to the fact that OC spray was used on Mr. Martin. Fields had used it prior to our arrival in efforts to bring the situation under control. The, shot of spray, actually missed due to the struggle fields was unable to get the spray in the direction of subject's face. Both I and fields had bleeding wounds to our hands. These wounds though superficial, were as a direct result of resisence by the subjects. Both I and fields refused transport by EMS. Both subjects were attended to by EMS and no medical assistance was rendered and both refused transport by EMS. At this time approximately 5 minutes had passed and we had several RCSD units on scene. Captain's Scott and Pearson were both present and I took time to brief these most senior officers of what took place and our actions. Capt. Pearson made it very clear from the beginning that he has had prior dealings with at least the male half. He knew his name and acted in such a way that he was not surprised by both subjects' actions. Mr. Martin seemed familiar with Capt. Pearson and repeatedly asked to speak with him personally. It turns out that Capt. Pearson is one of the resident courtesy officers at the complex. Capt. Pearson took an understanding tone with Martin, but made it very clear that he, (Martin) had brought this upon himself. I noticed that a man I had passed on my way in, had been in the area from the beginning and may have seen most, if not all, of the altercation. I approached him and asked if he were willing to provide a written statement, "Pro or con", in regards to what he had seen. The man agreed and provided the statement and I gave the statement to Dep. Fields to place with his future case jacket I and the other officers began to complete the needed booking paperwork; once EMS cleared, due to not being needed. A discussion began as to what to do about Mrs. Martin's cell phone. Someone, I am not sure who, stated that it should probably go into evidence. This was due to the fact that Mrs. Martin was making accusations that it contained "Police brutality" pictures. Placing it into evidence made sense, due to the fact they were going to take the phone from her during booking at the jail. We wanted to turn the phone off, as to conserve battery power. That way, when the phone was revealed in court the alleged incriminating photos would be present. Our concern was in regard to a later prosecution date and the rules of evidence.

Of course there is no specific policy on such matters and we were simply trying to do our best, for all concerned. We gave Martin the option of getting her phone back, but informed her it would to be taken from her upon arrival to the jail. With this in mind, she would loose any credibility with the photos at a later date. She of course would be able to claim any number of nefarious scenarios of the RCSD in regards to what had happened to the pictures. We felt that by placing the phone into an evidence bag, in her presence, and leaving the bag sealed until such a necessary date, this would assist her with whatever cause she felt the pictures would validate. Mr. Martin at this time could over hear some of our discussion about the phone and became quite animated in the back of the patrol car. I asked what was wrong and he stated that they should just delete the photos. I asked why, and he stated that there may be suggestive or sexual in nature images of his wife on the phone. I gave him the option we will place it into evidence, or return the phone now, and they could delete any photos on the scene. I took his concerns to his wife, located in the other vehicle; she had no problem with any images that may be contained on the phone. We made the decision to place the phone into evidence and I instructed Fields to notate this activity in his report. We kept both subjects separate until the paddy wagon arrived and both individuals were transported to AGDC without further incident.

Conclusion:

This was an extremely volatile incident and events were taking place in mere seconds. The fact that things did not deteriorate further is evidence of the quick action of units on the scene, this could have gone terribly wrong. There was a large crowd on scene with one officer by himself trying his best to bring things to order. The actions of the subjects not only jeopardized the safety of the Deputy present and other units, but to a greater degree the innocent public. When ever you have an "Officer Needs assistance from all over the region run code to respond and the public, unaware of the situation, is put at risk. The only injuries sustained by anybody, were suffered by RCSD units. I feel that the injuries were as a direct result of trained officers trying to use the minimal amount of force needed to bring the situation under control. More force could have been used at the scene. Borrowing from our training and our rules of force, RCSD would have been well within the bounds, to the use, of several impact weapons, (i.e.) Baton or Tazer. OC had been attempted and was proven ineffective. No it was due to well trained officers', good leadership and cooler heads that the subjects, were not injured in any way.

> Master Deputy J.A. Clarke
> Region 2
> RCSD
> Given on this day: 28 October, 2005

Tashiana and I were booked for Disturbance of the Peace, Assualt on an Officer, and Noise Violation. When they called Tashiana to take her picture they didn't recognize her by the description because of how the officers exaggerated her height and weight. They said she was 6 feet, 175 pounds and she was only 5.5 feet, 125 pounds. Then they processed me into the system and put us in a cell. I couldn't believe I was in my military uniform behind bars for the color of my skin. It was the second most humiliating feeling in my life. The first was watching my wife get beat up as I was handcuffed and couldn't do anything to protect her. We got out on bail and Jerod's mother (Sherri Lewis) picked us up and took us home.

That morning we went to Moncrief ER to be evaluate and they could still smell the pepper spray in my uniform and hair. I had cut and bruises all over me and my ribs and back was sore from being slammed to the ground, punched and kicked. I immediately told 1SG Peterman who was over my unit at Moncrief hospital. He knew I was a good soldier because I just finish being soldier of the month and I was winning trophies for our company for unit sports. I was the best flag football player on Ft. Jackson.

We went back to the police station to speak with Internal Affairs about how we were wrongfully abused by the Richland County Police Department. We sat down and answered questions with the people from Internal Affairs. Officer Benjamin Field was so cocky he even admitted to all of the racist comments he made to me. I was astonished he didn't lie about his racist comments, but when you're used to getting away with abusing the public, why would you be afraid? Once we received the Internal Affairs report I took it back to my unit so they could see that I wasn't lying. My mother had already been notified and was deeply hurt that she could dedicate her life to the military for 24 years for racism to still exist. All the sacrifice she had done for the military to uphold the laws of the United States for equality.

Internal Affairs Report of Sherri Lewis:

Q: Internal Affairs

A: Sherri Lewis

Q: On 10/24/05, where did you first see Mr. Martin?

A: I was sitting on my back porch and I saw him pass by

Q: Approximately how far away were you from him at that time?

A: Probably 50 yards maybe

Q: What was he driving?

A: He was driving his white SUV

Q: When you saw him did you hear any music?

A: No

Q: When was the next time you saw him?

A: After my son came and got me he told me the Police had Carlos and he needed help

Q: Prior to your son telling you the police had Carlos, did you hearing yelling or profanity coming from the parking lot?

A: No. I was in the back

Q: Where was Carlos when you saw him?

A: He was lying on the ground face down and the police was on top of him

Q: Was Carlos struggling in anyway?

A: It seemed to me he was just trying to turn his head. He was yelling for someone to get his wife.

Q: What was the officer doing when he was on top of Carlos?

A: He was on top of Carlos with both knees. He had hold of one arm far as I could see

Q: Did you see the officer spray Carlos?

A: Yes

Q: How many people were watching this?

A: Ms. Goins, my son and me. His wife was also there

Q: Did you witness the arrest of Mrs. Martin?

A: Yes

Q: In your statement you said the officer handcuffed her and slammed her to the ground?

A: Right

Q: Are you sure she was handcuffed prior to being slammed to the ground?

A: Yes

Q: Was she handcuffed behind her back?

A: She was

Q: When you say ground, do you mean the pavement?

A: Right

Q: Was she handcuffed behind her back?

A: She was

Q: Can you describe the officer who slammed her to the pavement?

A: He was tall, bald on top, sort of pale

Q: Was he a large man?

A: Right

Q: Would you say he was much larger than Mrs. Martin?

A: Oh yeah, by a lot

Q: Can you tell me how a large officer, much bigger than Mrs. Martin, can slam her on the pavement with the handcuffs behind her back, and she not have a scratch on her?

A: No

Q: How far away were you from the arrest of handcuffing of Mrs. Martin?

A: I was right next to them, within a couple of feet

Q: What did you say if anything when you saw them?

.A: I said, "Oh my God, wait."

Q: At what point did the officer approach you and push you?

A: Right after my comment

Q: At that time are you still within a couple of feet of Mrs. Martin and the officers?

A: Right

Q: You did not witness the initial contact the officer had with Mr. Martin prior to you seeing him on the ground, do you know for a fact Mr. Martin did not resist prior to your arrival?

.A: I don't know

Q: Can you identify the officer who handcuffed Mrs. Martin?
A: I think so
Q: In showing you a picture of Dep. Fields, is this the officer who handcuffed Mrs. Martin?
A: No

Internal Affairs Report of Ruthie Fay:
Q: Internal Affairs
A: Ruthie Fay
Q: Prior to seeing Mr. Martin and the deputy outside your apartment, did you hear any loud music?
A: No, I did not hear any loud music
Q: When you saw the deputy and Mr. Martin talking, did you hear either one of them yelling or using profanity?
A: No I didn't. When looked out I saw Mr. Martin handing the deputy something
Q: Did you see Mr. Martin and the deputy engage in some type of struggle?
A: Whatever was said it looked like it made the deputy angry. I went downstairs and the deputy had Mr. Martin on the ground
Q: You don't know if there was some type of struggle prior to you getting downstairs?
A: No, I don't know what happened between that time.

Q: Was Mrs. Martin yelling and using profanity towards the deputies prior to them arresting her?

A: She was yelling and using a couple of choice words

Q: Is that when they arrested her?

A: Yeah

Q: When did they put the handcuffs on Mrs. Martin?

A: I think it was when she was on the ground

Q: How close was the lady holding the puppy to Mrs. Martin when they arrested her?

A: I don't know how close, she was yelling at them, "Don't do that RICHLAND COUNTY SHERIFF'S DEPARTMENT!"

Some people should not be cops because they have mental issues or PTSD. Does he have trouble sleeping, anxiety, nightmares, cold sweats, family issues, flashbacks, road rage, bipolar, depression, withdrawal, avoidance, repression, emotional numbing, irritability?

Why would he be so angry? How many times a year do officers have to pass a psychological test to see if they are stable? As a civilian we can't get mad and beat up some guy and his wife on the street without facing charges over words. What happens to his police training because all police officers don't conduct themselves in this manner. You have some officers that want to do the right thing and make a difference and they follow their training. They know how to keep their cool and analyze a situation without abusing their power. Thank you to all the officers who stand up for what is right and make a difference in our communities.

Chapter 5

I Guess All Soldiers Don't Bleed Green

I called Colonel Jenkins, who was the commander of Ft. Richardson in Alaska, and reached out for help. He referred me to Todd Rudderford and we went to him to seek representation. When we met, we told him about the case. He thought we had a strong case, but we couldn't afford him.

I returned to work and went to the JAG office for representation. They couldn't help me since we were jumped by the police outside of post. I reached out to Judy Gaston, a news reporter for WIS, for help. She ran the story by her people, but they refused to run our story. We went to Ireport.com to share what happened to us with CNN. We reached out to Mr. Randle from the NAACP branch in South Carolina and they refused to help us. Their only concern were donations.

I contacted Jesse Jackson's organization and they wouldn't help us either. It really pissed me off that these NAACP branches hid under their names to collect money from people. I reached out to Congressman Clydeborn and they called my job a couple of times, but nothing really happened to my knowledge. I wrote my Congressman Don Young. He helped me so much and I'm so grateful to him. He wrote letters and emails and kept me from going to Korea so I could stand trial and fight my case.

I met with Command Sergeant Major (CSM) Phyllis Joseph, who was a Black woman, and told her what happened to me. Her response was so outrageous and disrespectful to me as a soldier and person. She told me that I was young and black and deserved what happened to me. She said, "You're nothing but a young Black hood rat. Why would the police do that to you? What's so special about you that I should believe your word over the police?" This was definitely a wakeup call for me. There is a thin line between loyalty and reality. I thought we all wore green and that we were supposed to have each other's back, especially when a person is telling the truth.

I have won so many trophies and Soldier of the Month boards and awards, and it didn't mean anything. I went from being the Most Valuable Player to the Rodney King of the hospital. We had not been found guilty on any charges yet, but I was being treated as if I was guilty. 1SG Peterman came down on orders to go to a new duty station and his replacement was 1SG Walls. Sometimes when a person takes over a new position of power they try to showcase their power by making an example out of someone. So, when the new 1SG took over, she neglected the truth and flagged me, stopped me from getting promoted, kicked me off the sports team, gave me my 1st Article 15, and had me doing extra duty after work. I had to cut grass and pick up trash before and after work. I couldn't understand why the military turned its back on me. It really sent me into a depression. I was innocent and being wrongfully treated because of the color of my skin.

As I was reaching out to everyone for help I remembered the old saying: What goes up must come back down. The more help I tried to get the more I got blackballed by the Army. I worked in the Patient Administration division and my fellow non-commission officers turned their backs on me. I don't know if they wanted to treat me unfairly or if there was pressure coming from CSM Joseph and 1SG Walls, forcing them to make the choice to save themselves or punish me. It got so bad I started to write a log of different events that happened to me while I was at work.

11 DEC 07 Email written by Major (MAJ) Fine to help me meet with Col. Mundy.

BLUF: "Sgt. Martin is trying to have his PCS orders deleted to ROK with a report date of 8 Jan 08. He requests an "open door policy" office call with Col. Mundy. Sgt. Martin is pending a felony charge in South Carolina. He feels strongly that with a jury trial he will be found not guilty. South Carolina is not negotiating, but they are stalling most likely due to the fact that Sgt. Martin has filed a civil suit against the law enforcement agency that arrested both he and his wife for resisting arrest for a charge of disturbing the peace and a noise violation.

The disturbing the peace and noise violation has been dismissed against both individuals. Sgt. Martin's suit is based upon his treatment by Richland County deputies (Violation of his Civil Rights). Civil rights cases are heard in the U.S. federal courts. The pending resisting arrest charge is via South Carolina court system. The Army can PCS Sgt. Martin based on Captain Roton's (the new JAG for MACH) legal opinion. Sgt. Martin is on PCS orders to Korea with a report date of 10 Jan 08. His private lawyers have advised him that it is in his interest to remain in South Carolina to the fight case. The South Carolina court order applies to him and his wife." (End of email)

CSM Joseph told Sergeant First Class (SFC) Moody my orders were not approved by Col. Mundy, which is not true. I have a military form with Col. Mundy's signature approving it. I don't understand why I couldn't get on the colonel's calendar to use the open door policy when CSM told me on 22 Nov 07 that she would set up an appointment but I'm glad that Major Fine sent that email out.

On 22 Nov 07, I went to Mrs. Jones' office to set an appointment with Col. Mundy using his open door policy. I spoke with SFC Moody and Captain Almond to let them know that I would like to speak to Col. Mundy. CSM Joseph told me she would make an appointment with Col. Mundy for me but according to Col. Mundy's secretary CSM Joseph did no such thing.

29 Nov 07 at 1000, after Staff Sergeant (SSG) Adams' reenlistment I checked on my appointment with Col. Mundy. CSM Joseph called me in her office with Master Sergeant (MSG) Stribbling and told me she was sick of me and sick of answering JAG questions concerning my situation. CSM Joseph called me a HOOD RAT, which was totally unprofessional! I told her I was not a HOOD RAT. She said people call her a BITCH and that she is a BITCH. If she feels that way about herself, it doesn't give her the right to address me in that fashion. She asked me, "Why are you trying to make a civil issue into a military issue?" She told me if I kept trying to get out of my orders to Korea, I was going to force her to do her job. She was going to flag me, take my rank and money and make sure I PCS (orders to a new duty station) to Korea. If I got out of my orders, she was going to put me out of the Army. I had not committed any crime and I was really scared and nervous about what my CSM could do to my career.

On 12 Dec 07, I met with Col. Mundy about 1630. While in his office I felt as if CSM Joseph put a threat on my life because when we were in the office with MSG Stribbling she said she was going to make sure I PCS. When she found out my orders were deleted, she called me selfish and stated that every time a soldier dies in Iraq she is going to think it should have been me because I didn't PCS to Korea! This is coming from my Senior NCO, my leader. I find that comment disrespectful to the soldiers who have given their lives for our country. I couldn't believe that CSM would say that to me.

On 13 December 2007, This was a lot of stress in my life. I had to deal with the stress of my court case. As if that wasn't enough, I had to deal with the pressure of my CSM threatening to end my career.

I would bring my lunch to work and they would throw my lunch away. It was a war zone going to work. I was public enemy No. 1 because I was willing to fight for my rights. Why is it when a person stands for the right thing that everyone else becomes so hateful? Are they mad at you or are they mad at themselves because you're doing what they wish they had the guts to do for themselves?

Viewpoint of Co-Worker W. C. Leonard, Moncrief Army Health Clinic:

"First off, the initial police brutality took place when Rodney King was beaten. His case went to court and he was award a small victory. However, fast forward to the last decade the police brutality or violence has escalated to more than a beating. It has evolved into senseless shooting of black men in America. I feel like police violence will continue at an all-time high, simply because there has been no conviction of any officers who have pulled the trigger and killed a black male. When Charles Kinsey, a mental health therapist, was shot protecting his white autistic patient asked, 'Why did you shoot me?' The officer said, 'I do not know.' I'm sorry IDK is not enough.

It affects the family, because the family has lost a 'loved one.' It doesn't matter what age the individual is, all that matters is a family member is cut down in the streets like an animal. Second, if the victim was the 'bread winner' of the family, it will definitely bring hard times on the surviving family. It promotes fear for the surviving family members and raises the question, can cops and the justice system be trusted to be impartial.

What can be done to resolve police violence?

- ☐ Protest the city halls, police departments, local governments, and Washington
- ☐ Mental health backgrounds on all officers
- ☐ Conduct mandatory social justice training
- ☐ Start police community patrol teams
- ☐ Ban excessive deadly force
- ☐ Remove police from schools
- ☐ Know your rights when interacting with law enforcement.

As an individual, you were the type of person I could trust and call my brother in Christ, my family without question. Personally, I thought you were an outstanding soldier (NCO). You displayed leadership and the Army values toward your fellow soldiers. You showed camaraderie within the office amongst the team of soldiers and civilians. In my opinion, the Army handled your situation as if they were trying not to bring exposure to them, as if they were the assailants. The department treated you like you did not belong here, and was willing to deport you to another section (if you catch what I am saying). CSM Joseph gave you a bad report, saying you deserved that and you had it coming. The Army and the organization failed you as soldier and a citizen.

The officer who violated your civil rights was Officer Ben Fields, of the Richland County Sheriff's Department. It could have been handled differently if the officer who arrested you would not have committed himself to racial profiling you. If he would have just questioned you about what he was looking for in the first place, since you were just coming home, while he was patrolling your housing community.

Yes, I think we can have equality if voters get out and vote for the candidate of their choosing. Hopefully, they have done their homework on the candidate prior to the election and stopped to pay attention to TV ads and town halls…dig deeper into the candidate's family background. A candidate will say anything to get votes. Law enforcement needs training similar to the military. They are not that different.

If you were white, do I think the police would have handled you different? I say yes…it is my believe that personnel tries to repeat what others can get away with, i.e. copycat. If the rest of the nation have not convicted a white cop for brutalizing or killing a black male, they test the waters. Now with the army organization that you were in, I think it was all about how your section viewed you as a soldier first, and an individual second. However, if you had the favor of CSM Joseph, who was the senior enlisted soldier in this organization, it might have been different."

Chapter 6

Fighting for Our Freedom

During our search for a lawyer we came across John Mobley. We went downtown to his office to see if he was willing to represent us. I was happy to see a Black lawyer because I assumed that he would understand what it's like to be a black man in America. We sat down with him, explained our case, and showed him the internal affairs reports. He was willing to represent us and it was going to cost somewhere in the neighborhood of $10,000. I didn't have that kind of money. So, I called my mom and asked if she was willing to lend it to me and we would pay her back. We also called Tashiana's family, but they didn't have the money to help my mom out. So, my mom paid for everything. This started a feud between our families, despite the fact they were all happy we were okay.

John Mobley became our lawyer and he started building a case to defend us. We asked how much did he thought we could win in a case like this? He said he wasn't sure and it depended on the injuries, pain and suffering, medical records and damages. I asked if he thought we had a million dollar lawsuit and responded that we might but he couldn't promise anything. He stated we had a strong case and the good thing is he believed us. Every time he asked us questions, we always responded with the same answers. I told him how I reached out to the media, NAACP, Rainbow Push, Judi Gaston, White House, etc.

I couldn't find peace because I had to deal with pressure from family fighting. My mom paid $10,000 for us to hire a lawyer to represent us so we wouldn't go to jail and, at the time, Tashiana's family couldn't help. We were receiving threats from the Richland County Police Department while we were living at Quail Run. So, we decided to move to Polo Commons, but they still found us there. The police would come and knock on our doors and fake like they were looking for someone else, just to see if we lived there. They could have gotten that information from the business office. We were scared to drive because if we were pulled over by a cop they could run our information and know exactly who we were.

I wound up getting kicked out of the hospital because it was a hostile work environment. SFC Stinney and SSG Lindo were in charge of me now and I answered to them. I told them about my situation and showed them all of the documents I had been keeping.

Sometimes in life when people try to put you in a worse situation, it's actually a blessing in disguise.

I had to see a psychologist to talk about what happened to me and my family. Tashiana and I were going through a divorce. She felt like I couldn't protect her and she was traumatized by the event. I didn't feel like a man anymore because I couldn't protect her. It felt like all of Ben Fields' threats came true. We faced anxiety, fear, depression and lack of money at every turn.

This felt like a bottomless pit of poison that we couldn't handle, in addition to facing 10 years in jail. Tashiana was in school studying to become a nurse, but you can't be a nurse with a felony charge. It was as if she was going to school for nothing. All of her hard work could have been taken from her because of the color of her skin. I was fighting to be a soldier, had to pay mother back, was facing 10 years, and trying to protect us from the police who continued to harass us. What was the right way to deal with the situation? Should we just let it go and let Officer Ben Fields and Officer Joseph Clarke get way with what they did? The advice we were receiving from everyone on a daily basis was crazy. It was just suffocating and we couldn't breathe.

During this time my mom was also writing a book called *What Mommies Need to Know*. She was having a book signing at the VA hospital and that's where she met a gentleman named Earl Graham. Earl was working with a group called *Police Abuse* with Diop Kamau and his wife Miss Jackson.

My Mom's Perspective on How She Met Earl Graham

Earl was telling us that Mr. Kamau could really help Carlos with this situation because he also went through some things with Richland County. So, it was very unique and special to have met Mr. Earl Graham. I felt like there was finally some relief for my son and the issues he was going through, which gravely impacted our family. In particular, as his mom and him being my youngest son joining the Army. I know he was following in my footsteps. I just did not expect the army command to treat my son the way they had.

Well, Earl had us on these weekly, sometimes daily calls where we would be processing everybody's case from all across the country as a result of police abuse. Mr. Graham became a very good friend of my son because he also was having an issue with Richland County. I remember when Earl and I would go and

Kamau had all of us investigating and making calls to the police department to learn their policies and procedures. I can recall the time when Leon Lott the sheriff, who's still the sheriff, would tell me not to call the sheriff's department anymore. I just felt really hopeless. Mr. Graham always seemed to provide some kind of hope for us to let us know it was okay and everything was going to work out in our favor. I remember one time when I went with an investigator to talk to the sheriff's department or Internal Affairs to gather information and data. It was a hush-hush thing and as a mother it really did bother me because I didn't want anything to happen to my son. What happened to my son was completely unfair. It bothered me because I also felt helpless and I had to be on the road.

As a mother as a first sergeant in the United States Army, I understood the problems he was experiencing, but I didn't understand why the chain of command was treating my son the way they had. I later learned that the solicitor, or soon-to-be outgoing solicitor, worked for Richland County as well as the military. So, there was no way my son was going to get a fair chance in the Army because Richland County had somebody on the inside.

Here we had this young innocent soldier that was being mistreated on a daily basis, literally breaking down and crying, but he always kept hope. That's one thing I'll say about my son, Carlos. He always had hope and kept hope alive. He became an advocate fighting for those who were mistreated by the police. My son was scarred mentally, emotionally, and physically. He had issues even within his marriage. That's the part that really hurt me to watch a young soldier, in this particular case my young soldier, be treated that way for no reason. All because this prejudice cop had a problem with my son calling him a "dude."

I moved to South Carolina to help my son Carlos. Our family had been going through a lot of traumatic things. I was driving back and forth from Virginia to South Carolina to be a support to my son. He was having a meltdown, a breakdown, as a result of a divorce stemming from the incident that compounded many other things. I wanted my son to know he was not alone. It was time for me to retire from the military so I was okay with relocating to South Carolina.

It was also a blessing to be able to have the money to help my son, because I knew my son was innocent. So, for me to spend over seventy-five hundred dollars for an attorney for my son, was peanuts. My husband Andre had passed away and there was available to be a blessing to my son and his wife to help them get an attorney. We paid the attorney, John Mobley, on the spot. I will never forget him, but my son stayed on a personal recognizance bond for three years, which I did not understand. It really bothered me that my son went through these things after paying an attorney just to learn later that the same attorney was in cahoots with the judicial system.

As a mother watching her child go through these things was very stressful, but it made me know I had raised my son right. While he was being beaten, he told me he was praying on the ground. He was telling his wife the Lord was going take care it. I raised my son to depend on the Lord, but I did not raise my son to be beaten by cops, white cops, black cops, any kind of cop for no reason. I was thankful the Taser didn't show up and I was grateful the rookie cop didn't pull a gun on my son. Yet I was very disheartened and disappointed that my family was experiencing a soldier serving in the United States Army being treated this way. He was a young black male who had pride and was not afraid to stand up for himself. That made him a threat to those officers. Officer Joe Clarke was a failure to me, especially as a supervisor. Not only did he not stop the situation from escalating, but he poured gasoline on the fire by attacking a woman who was not a threat to him. It bothered me because I could immediately see racism and prejudice take its course and raise its ugly head, and it didn't matter.

A few months later, my heart went out to Trayvon Martin, because my son's name is Carlos Martin. All I could do was grieve for that mother, but at the same time, I was very grate and thankful that nothing happened to my son, Carlos.

I'm proud of Carlos right now. He's been through a lot. I'm grateful God has kept him, and I know He has greater things in store for him. I'm excited about Carlos wanting to publish his story. My son is a phenomenal young man, and I'm grateful to God for being his mom.

My Mom's Email to Sheriff Lott:

Sheriff Leon Lott,
My name is Shirley Martin Flowers. I am a retired, disabled veteran, concerned citizen, and parent.
On 28 March 2011, I received a call from your Internal Affairs Office. The individual calling identified himself as a Lieutenant Padgett. Lt. Padgett stated that IA was not going to investigate my written complaint filed in their office on or about 25 March 2011. I also called Chief Burkheimer, your chief, inquiring why this decision was made since Lt. Padgett

said he had made the decision. After a long and uneventful conversation with the chief, I found his reasons unacceptable concerning this matter and he referred me to you at my request. I am not certain why you called me yesterday but I was unavailable at the time to talk to you.

Bottom line Leon, I provided a written request to your IA office. I am appalled that your agency finds it acceptable to make a phone call to answer a formal written complaint. I am requesting a formal response back to me in writing indicating why you have opted not to investigate my complaint. The case in question involves Deputy Ben Fields, an incompetent officer who racially profiled, beat and maced Sgt. Carlos Martin while illegally arresting him.

Officer Joe Clarke, his senior officer, was present at the scene and condoned this behavior. In fact he told the witness that he "would take their black asses to jail if they don't get back." The witnesses were not interfering but were witnessing their inappropriate actions. As a senior officer, he chose to cover up this racist, inappropriate action instead of taking charge to make the right decision. Sgt. Martin was not only treated wrongly because of his race but his civil rights were violated by both officers.

Sgt. Martin was assigned to Fort Jackson, SC to continue serving our country, providing freedom and justice for all. In fact, he and his wife had just returned from overseas fighting to get beat up on American soil by a racist cop. Sgt. Martin's military service actually provided the opportunity for Ben Fields, Joe Clarke, Chief Berkheimer, Lt. Padgett, and you to properly serve and protect the citizens of Richland County.

I am not stating that all your officers are incompetent but I am stating that Ben Fields and Joe Clarke failed to provide competency during this incident. Now I am being denied the right as a citizen to file an IA complaint by Lt. Padgett and Chief Berkheimer.

Not only have the above incidents occurred, but the racial profiling, beating and harassment were reported to the Staff Judge Advocate Office at Fort Jackson. Chief Daniel Johnson advised Sgt. Martin to drop his case against Richland County. Sgt. Martin was told that if he drops the charges your office would drop their case (Felony Assault Against An Officer) against Sgt. Martin. This advice was suggested and recommended by Johnson and Sgt. Martin's chain of command.

Unknowingly to Sgt. Martin, Chief Johnson worked for both the military and Richland County Sheriff Department at that time. There was no way Chief Johnson could perform his duties unbiasly. Chief Johnson actually confirmed Officer Fields' statement, "that he is a Richland County Deputy and he can get away with whatever he wanted" while beating Sgt. Martin.

Ben Fields had a person on the inside of the judicial system at Fort Jackson and RCSD. Of course we did not drop our case. Sgt. Martin and his now ex-wife, also a disabled veteran, were found innocent of all false charges filed by Ben Fields and Joe Clarke to cover up their racist actions. For racially motivated reasons, Fields and Clarke beat a soldier in military uniform, used racial slurs toward innocent bystanders and violated the victims' civil rights.

Neither officer could justify their actions as decided by the Honorable Judge Renee Lee while lying during their testimony under oath. The Martins were given a direct verdict of innocence. I am now hearing that you are forwarding all Internal Affairs complaints to SLED Director Reggie Lloyd. I am requesting for you to clarify if this is true or not. Finally, Chief Berkheimer indicated that you could provide information as to whether or not these officers were disciplined for their inappropriate actions.

I am further requesting you to disclose what disciplinary actions were taken against Deputy Ben Fields and Deputy Joe Clarke, if any. I am now personally requesting to file a complaint against Deputy Ben Fields, Deputy Joe Clarke, Lt. Padgett, and Chief Berkheimer.

Sincerely,

Shirley Martin Flowers

1SG (Retired)

USA

Concerned Citizen

Chapter 7

Joining Police Abuse

Earl Graham was a veteran who served in the United States Army. One day while waiting for one of his appointments at the V.A. Medical Center in Columbia, South Carolina he ran into my mother, who was conducting a book signing. She asked him about his military career and Earl told her that he served.

They began talking about Ft. Richardson in Alaska and he found out she just left Alaska. He asked her if she new a young man named Colonel Jenkins. My mother replied with a big smile and said, "Absolutely, he was my commander at Ft Richardson in Alaska. I was good friends with his son Chris, Jr." When Earl realized she knew Chris Jenkins, his demeanor changed and his defensives went down immediately. That was the beginning of a beautiful friendship that would last for years.

My mom came home and told me about her meeting Earl Graham and that he was a part of a group called *Police Abuse*. She said they wanted to help me with my case against Richland County. We joined the conference call and spoke with others who had cases against the police. Mr. Kamau and his wife allowed us to join *Police Abuse* and we became a part of the *Police Abuse* family.

Earl Graham's Perspective on How He Met My Mom and How He Introduced Me to Police Abuse

After discussing military events, we started talking about politics and things that were happening in Columbia, South Carolina. She (Miss Flowers) just so happened to mention that her son (Carlos) got into a situation with one of the local law enforcement individuals who worked for the Sheriff's Department. As I was listening, little did she know that I was in a similar situation myself. I was dealing with an organization by the name of *Police Abuse* out of Tallahassee, Florida that had come up to the Columbia area and was investigating the sheriff's department for abuse and neglect of African-Americans in Richland County.

From there, I learned that Carlos, her son, was attacked by an individual who was the same officer promoted to be over children at Spring Valley High School. This police deputy's name was Ben Fields. This was approximately 2009. Ben Fields was promoted to resource officer at Spring Valley High School. Once they realized it was Officer Fields, Carlos and Miss Flowers linked up with Police Abuse.

I got him in touch with Diop Kamau. Kamau agreed to take the case and started working with the numerous individuals we had in the group. The group stemmed from individuals who were beaten by police officers to individuals who were sexually assaulted. Once we had the opportunity to hear the full story of Carlos Martin we found out that his case was very similar to mine because they had the same players, Leon Lott and Dan Johnson. Dan Johnson just so happened to be a JAG officer at Ft. Jackson, which was considered to be his additional duty in the Army Reserves. Johnson was also a Richland County Deputy Sheriff, second in charge as the Chief Deputy under Richland County Sheriff Leon Lott.

The confrontation Johnson had and the advice he was rendering while in uniform was very misleading and controversial because he was holding down a civilian job as a cop and a military job as a JAG officer. He gave advice to Carlos Martin concerning his situation that took place with Ben Fields, knowing full well that Fields worked directly for him as one of the resource officers during his day job as the Richland County Chief Deputy Sheriff. Again, this was a conflict of interest. Needless to say, Johnson not only abused Mr. Martin, but he abused me and my children later on by pulling things that were extremely unethical in his position as the Chief Deputy of Richland County, South Carolina.

Once Mr. Kamau got involved with the Martin family, Carlos came into the picture and started working with the group to give advice and assist individuals with their cases while we were dealing with background information surrounding his assault.

Chapter 8

Facing 10 Years in Jail and the Army vs. Freedom

We had to go through hours on top of hours of depositions as part of our case. There was much sitting at a table and the only thing they really gave us was water while they played good cop, bad cop. The truth never changes so know matter how they continued to change the same questions over and over again it remained the same. They would take parts of what you said and rearrange it to make you feel like you're going crazy. They would do this process until they wore you down just to make you change your answers to make it seem as if you're a liar. I'm talking about emotional and mental abuse. This is a perfect example of how you can wear someone down to try to make them say what you want them to say. After the depositions were over, the police continued to harass us leading up to the court date.

It took four years for us to finally go to court. We were so nervous because we knew that we were not guilty of anything but being a minority in America you're already considered guilty. Some consider blacks only three-fifths of a person. Despite being threatened by the military not to wear my uniform in court I wore it anyway. I didn't understand how they could tell me that I couldn't wear my uniform to court but it was okay for the Richland County police officers to assault me in my military uniform.

I saw these young brothers in the courtroom waiting for their case to be called. They were acting as if the courtroom was a family reunion or a club. They were laughing about the last time they saw each other in the court and bragging about how many charges they had, as if it was a badge of honor. It literally broke my heart because of their views of life and being black in America. I told them that being in court is nothing to brag about and I'm not putting my life on the line for them just so they could throw theirs away. I said people are listening and watching you. It's embarrassing for officers who are fighting to make a better way for our people.

Harriet Tubman said she freed 1,000 slaves but she could have freed 1,000 more if they knew they were slaves. How true is her statement today? How do we buy into the BS as a culture and forget who we are? What was our price? The young men could respect where I was coming from because I came from a place of love. I wanted our people to do better. Regardless of the circumstances thrown at us,

124

Facing 10 Years in Jail and the Army vs. Freedom

we still have a choice to be powerful, united and love each other.

Our family was in the courtroom and I remembered the truth will set you free and the truth never changes. So when we took the stand we had to raise our hand and swear to tell the truth, and nothing but the truth, so help you GOD. Nothing in our stories changed no matter how many times they asked us questions.

When officer Ben Fields took the stand and swore to tell the truth and nothing but the truth things got really interesting. Mr. Mobley went through his opening statement, telling the jury how we were innocent and that Officer Fields' history showed that he was cop with an attitude who attacked us. While questioning Officer Ben Fields we had the internal affairs report where he previously answered questions about wrongfully assaulting us and all the racial comments he made. So when Mr. Mobley questioned him he asked questions from the internal affairs statement, which is a legal document that could be used against him in the court of law. He lied about everything he previously admitted to in the internal affairs report. Our lawyer asked him to read the report out loud to the jury.

The judge was baffled at how he kept lying on the stand and she was going to hold him in contempt of court. He would say things like he didn't recall but if that is what it says then it must be true. The judge nearly cried and apologized to our family because of the ignorance and cockiness of officer Ben Fields and Joseph Clarke. She dismissed the case with the highest verdict of non guilty that you could receive.

My fellow NCO Sgt. Marshall came to the courthouse to report what happened in our case. She immediately walked out and went back to the Army base to inform them that we were not guilty and they totally screwed me over. Marshall was a good NCO and she looked out for me, giving me advice throughout my career after I first met her in Germany. She just had to do what she had to do in her position. Sometimes people don't want to do something but they are forced to choose between their ethics or survival for themselves.

When it was time for us to go to court for our lawsuit I was deceived by my lawyer. He convinced me to drop the battery charge that I had against the police. He said we were going to win on all these other charges and that he would represent us free of charge. I told him that I didn't understand why I needed to drop the battery charge when it was part of my claim and why was he in such a rush to get me to sign it. I told him that I wanted to call my mother because this didn't make sense to me.

126

Facing 10 Years in Jail and the Army vs. Freedom

I knew my mom had paid $10,000 and we didn't have the money to pay for another attorney after we won the criminal case. I made sure he understood I didn't agree with it but that if he was going to represent us in court I would sign it. I wasn't familiar with this because I had never been in trouble with the law. I didn't fully understand the system and how it worked.

As soon as I signed that paper he faxed it in. Then he turned around and said he was going to charge my family double. We were fighting the court system and now the attorney who just helped us win in court. So, my charges against the police got dropped despite the fact I appealed to a higher court. I actually filed paperwork with the United States Supreme Court and I'm still waiting for my case to be heard.

My ex went to court, but she was being represented by a different attorney. They didn't allow me to be a part of her court case. She was so tired of fighting because she just wanted to get back to having a normal life. They knew we were going through a divorce at the time so they used it against us to prevent us from winning our civil suit. I was told that I couldn't come to her trial, but I went anyway. It was so crazy because the judge admitted he knew the head juror. The judge stated that the head juror's dad helped build the courthouse. I could have sworn that the judge was not supposed to know anyone in the jury and it was against the law.

My ex lost her case because they said that she was too close to the police officer when she was taking pictures. You can clearly see that was a lie by the remaining pictures that were left after the officer tampered with the evidence.

We were found not guilty on all charges, which means we did nothing wrong. We went to the next court and the judge overturned what the other judge ruled. If we didn't do anything wrong why were we assaulted by the police? Why were we taken and booked? Why did we have to pay for lawyers? How did I lose my military career and my marriage? What happened to being compensated for mental and physical damages?

She was tired of fighting, our divorce was done, and I continued to fight this fight by myself.

After court I went back to the Army to go through my medical board evaluation. I never got a fair evaluation because I wrote to Congressman Don Young about my work environment. The people I wrote my congressional letter about were the same people who did my medical evaluation. There was no way they were going to give me a fair medical review. I was supposed to have surgery on my ACL but Dr. Eslava was told he wasn't allowed to do my surgery. I believe it was because they

128

Facing 10 Years in Jail and the Army vs. Freedom

knew they messed up and a lot of people could have lost rank in the Army and civilians would have lost their jobs.

When you're in the military and you're injured, you get down-time for recovery. For example, two months would be four months time to recover from your situation. They couldn't discharge me from the military because I was in recovery phase. The longer I was in the military the more they were exposed and the more people would continue asking questions.

I should have been evaluated on a different Army base or civilian hospital to get a fair medical review. I was going through the process of being put out by the Army. I received a 0% medical retirement because of the Command Sergeant Major, 1SG, MSG of Patient Administration Division, and the people over the medical board office.

I called and told my mother and we decided to send a package to the White House with all the documents. It revealed how the military wrongfully handled my case. It contained a letter to Congressman Don Young and the paperwork showing I reached out to the NAACP and RAINBOW PUSH.

We made copies of the packet and took it to the Post Commander of South Carolina. We informed him about what happened and how I was wrongfully treated and showed the Post Office stamp that was sent to the White House. He went over the documents and my medical board review. My medical rating was changed from 0% to 70% by the same people who initially gave me 0%. I felt like I was finally being heard and things were moving in the right direction. Then they dropped me back to 30% for my retirement. The VA was scared of my case because of how high it went up and the names that were attached to it.

I ended up getting an honorable discharge from the military with a 70% rating but I had a re-evaluation in six months. When I went back to go get re-evaluated they dropped my retirement from 70% to 30%. Any soldier who has to go through the VA process understands my pain of getting appointments and how long they take. They understand the War on Friendly Grounds to receive VA benefits they are entitled to after putting their lives on the line for this country. The VA is so backlogged it takes forever to get a case reviewed. There are amazing people at the VA who work hard and I appreciate what they do, but the system definitely needs to be upgraded.

Chapter 9

The Spark to My Flame

My mom saw that I was in a dark place. So, she decided to invite me to CEO Space. CEO Space is a private entrepreneur club in Henderson, Nevada. I was very reluctant to go with her because I didn't want to be around people after losing everything. It was like my mind turned into a machine and I couldn't turn it off.

I kept thinking about how I lost my marriage. How did I lose my career as a soldier after putting my blood, sweat and tears into it for 10 years? I witnessed my friends going to work and I didn't have a job. I went from living with my wife to living with my mother after living on my own for all those years. I was just Soldier of the Quarter and now I'm not a soldier at all. I won flag football trophies for my company and now I don't have a team to play for.

Everywhere I went I wondered if I was going to be killed by the police. The fact that I went from protecting my country to facing 10 years in jail because of the color of my skin. I went from taking terrorist calls for Jessica Lynch in Germany to being treated as if I were a terrorist. I spent more time with people that I worked with than my own family and they turned their backs on me so easily.

What did I do to deserve this? GOD, I'm a good person. How naïve was I to think the country I protected would protect me. I got treated better and felt like I was an equal in a place that was foreign to me. Is this American dream all bullshit? You grow up only seeing this one way of life, but when you finally leave this illusion that society has created for you, you see that everyone around the world just wants to be happy.

Why am I going to these appointments and talking to people who will never understand what I've been through? How can they tell you how to come out of something they never experienced themselves? They give generic tests that are preset by-the-book conversations. People can see that the building is on fire and feel bad for the people inside the building. But it's a different experience for the people inside the building. Then they want to drug you and act like your situation has changed. I have never seen a pill that stops racism so why do they keep wanting me to take all these drugs? That will never change the reality that I see on TV, Instagram, and Snapchat. How far have we fallen where we video people dying right in front of us and then post it for views. I understand some people do it for the right reason to get their story out.

Why do police officers get away with murder because they say they fear for their life? As if fear is the color blue and their lives are the only ones that matter. This horrible cycle of racism is not new in America because America was born out of it. Am I going crazy because it's the reality that we live in? How long have we been sitting in the boiling pot of poison where other people's lives don't matter anymore? How do we have a justice system that is so colorblind where two people can do the same crime and the color of your skin is a V.I.P. to freedom?

That's when I realized I was in the sunken place that America created. We all know that racism exists but yet we tend to operate on a day to day basis as if white privilege doesn't exist. Which led me to this thought: What makes a rainbow beautiful? Is it not the diversity of colors? If that is true do you think mankind's kryptonite is making one color better than the next, and if that happens is it still a rainbow? I think not! So why are we destroying something that GOD created, which is beautiful, with invisible lines of hate?

We are all six degrees of separation from loving each other and respecting each other's differences because we all want to be happy and successful. How did this hate come about and what is the root of it? How do we pull all the weeds of racism out of this garden of life? The Bible says, if man unites, we could accomplish anything. What type of world would it be if we were united? Is unity really that hard? I know Gandhi said self-discipline is the hardest discipline. Why do we have to look for a leader to make a change when the seed of change is planted already in our DNA? I truly believe that instead of looking at everyone else, we have to account for our own walk and mistakes. Share the love to make a difference one person at time.

So, I agreed to go to CEO Space. This lady walked up to me and asked, "How may I service you?" This is one of the greetings at CEO Space. I told her my name and that I had a medical invention I was thinking could be beneficial to everyone and their family. She smiled and touched me on my forehead and stomach and said, "My GOD, you really don't know who you are yet and what you have to give birth to." She asked me who was my favorite basketball player. I responded Kobe Bryant and named all of his stats. She said, "Wow, you know a lot about Kobe Bryant. What are your stats?"
She continued, "It's amazing how you can tell me about someone else's life but don't know your own life." That was mind-blowing and shocking to see how much attention I put on the

lives of others instead of what I needed to do for myself.

How much did they pay you to stop dreaming? Was it minimum wage, $15, $20? What plantation are you working for? Is it Google or McDonald's? There is no difference in the structure of a plantation or a business. On a plantation you have a slave, slave driver and master. In a business you have worker bees, managers and CEOs.

The lady told me to look around and tell her everything I see. So I looked around and told her I see a beautiful building, paintings, the clothes and shoes we had on. She stopped me and said everything I see is someone else's dream. She then proceeded to say that if I participate in everyone else's dream, who is participating in my dream? She asked me if my mom was a millionaire. I told her no. She asked me if I study money? I told her no and she replied how am I supposed to get something that I don't spend time with? She said, "Do you know the difference between wealthy and rich? Wealthy people have multiple avenues of income and will never have to work again. Most wealthy people look at minorities as jesters in the king's court. They dominate everything they do, but they don't own anything. So, Kobe may be able to leave his children five championship rings and the money he has made, but it's nothing like the owners who can leave their children five islands. Rich people have to continue to work to stay rich and maintain that lifestyle or appearance." I believe she was talking about me giving birth to this book that will be a blessing to the future.

When I left, another young lady came around the corner and talked to me. She also touched my forehead and said there was something special that I needed to do.
I told another lady it was interesting that it just happened again. She asked me who the other lady was. So, I described her and it turned out to be her mother, Myrna (A.K.A Goddess La Hottie). I also found out this lady named September was Mr. Berny's wife. Mr. Berny was the CEO of CEO Space.

I felt my life was starting over again because of these amazing people who enjoyed my medical invention. They saw the light in me even when I thought everything was taken from me. The forum was amazing and it was like I found my family all over again with some of the world's most successful people. I met Les Brown and his son John Leslie Brown, Bob Proctor of QVC, Jack Canfield of "Chicken Soup for Your Soul." I got to experience the magic of CEO Space. I was really good with young adults and very business savvy with all of the adults.

We created *Teen Space* and in less than 24 hours Gary Reid donated $500, which helped us get the logo and clothing design. It was nice to feel appreciated and loved again. I took all of Les Brown's platinum speakers and lined them up to tell their stories. There was this amazing young lady by the name of Pauline Aughe who spoke last. She was in a wheelchair with no arms and no legs. She said, "I have more 'I cans' than 'I cannot's!'" It was simply breathtaking to see someone in her situation smile so bright and have the integrity to live life to the fullest.

I realized how lucky I was to be alive because so many others in my situation were not here to tell their story. I met a young man named Marcale and he asked me what I thought about moving to California. Since I was having so much trouble in South Carolina maybe a change of scenery is what I needed. I thought about it. I have always wanted to be an actor. So, I decided to move to California. I went home and I talked to one of my best friends, Harold Thibodeaux, about moving to California. He was coming down on order and wanted me to watch his son Darion for him. I told him, "I got you." So Darion stayed with me while Tib was on assignment for the summer. When he returned, Tib fixed my truck by putting on new shocks, brakes, oil, and tires. Honestly, he was one of the few who believed in me.

So, I packed up my things and moved to California. There were so many haters when they found out I was moving to California to be an actor. I heard so many people say things like: your truck will never make it that far. What do you know about acting? You're a soldier and that's all you know. You just got beat up by the police and you think you can become a star. There are too many actors in L.A. already. Why would you want to go after a career that has such a high failure rate?

I went to California and decided to use my Post 911 G.I. bill to go to Heald College. I earned three associate degrees in Business Administration, Business Entrepreneurship, and Accounting because I wanted to make *Teen Space* official. The only problem with Teen Space was we had individuals who were age 14-22 in the group. So, we changed it to F.W.L., which stands for *Future World Leaders*.

While we were at Heald College, I created the first entrepreneur showcase where students in the class were able to showcase their business ideas. I had everything set up like the CEO Space. I invited speakers like Sherita Herring via Skype and Byron Nelson who came to the school to talk to the students about grants and becoming entrepreneurs. I went in front of the class and asked them if they would help me create the entrepreneur conference. We decided to call it N.E.N.A., which stood for the New Entrepreneur Network Association. It blew up so big and everyone wanted to be part of it but the school tried to steal my idea. I had to go to the principal's office (Mr. Frazier) and show him my business plan for F.W.L. proving that it was my idea. I told him how I stood before the class and asked them to help me with it. My teachers hid my sign that said I created N.E.N.A., but the crazy thing is after I graduated the school got shut down. Some people would say it was karma, but I didn't like the fact that my idea was stolen.

I went to John Casablanca, an acting and modeling school where I met with Francis and Dalena about becoming a professional actor. I took some classes there to help me get used to being in front of the camera and learn how to model. They sent me out to audition after taking my head shots and signed me up on Sfcasting.com. I signed up for auditions and started booking work. I auditioned for a Bank of America commercial and booked the job where we had to talk about finances. I got the role of a principal and they used my voice for the voice over. I didn't know how anything really worked because it was my first time booking a job.

A couple of weeks later my phone started blowing up like crazy with everyone saying they saw me on TV. I couldn't believe my commercial played during the World Series, NBA playoffs and the Super Bowl. That automatically made me eligible for SAG. So, I paid my dues and officially became a SAG actor.

I met a director named Ted Leonard and was a lead for the Discovery Channel show called *Wives With Knives* where I played the role of Carlton. I did another show called *Sex Sent Me to the Slammer,* and the episode was *Flatbed Floozy.*

A friend invited me to San Diego to audition for Mr. Mosley for the show *My Sweet Life with Zack and Cody.* There were so my many people there and I was like how can I make myself stand out to be different from everyone else? So, I picked up the lines they wanted me to do and I saw that it was a Pepsi commercial. I left the line and ran to the store to pick up a Pepsi to use in my audition.

When I got back they were calling my name to do the audition. So, I went in with an all-white outfit on with my motorcycle helmet. I introduced myself and started the audition. "What makes you cool? It's not your attitude. (I gave him a little attitude) It's not your haircut. (I set my motorcycle helmet down) It's not your clothes. (I took off my jacket) It's not what you drink, or is it?" I took the Pepsi I just bought out of my pocket. He smiled because he saw that I understood the script. I opened the Pepsi and it explodes all over me because I forgot that I was running back to the audition with it in my pocket. I stayed in character and said, "I guess I was just happy to see you." He caught my joke and laughed. He told me I needed to move to Hollywood. He said he loved my acting and I had a lot to offer Hollywood.

I moved to Burbank, California and continued my acting career. I met Carmen, who introduced me to Baron Brown, an acting school in Santa Monica. She also introduced me to Ronald Cuyler, who is having a successful career in Hollywood.

I was at home going over lines and life was amazing. I was working on my trauma and my acting career was taking off. I finished school and things were moving in the right direction.

The Spark to My Flame

Chapter 10

Facing Your PTSD

Why We Fear the Color Blue

I got a message from Sheldon Ferguson. I met Sheldon at a music video shoot. He attended Spring Valley High School, where the young lady was assaulted by Ben Fields. It was a video of an officer beating up a little girl in the classroom because she wanted to get up and leave the classroom. I immediately knew that it was Ben Fields and I wrote on the post that I knew this officer because he is the same officer who beat me and my ex up in front of my house.

It was like I was reliving everything that happened to us. I could feel the girl's pain and all I could think was if they would have handled it right in the first place that this officer wouldn't have the chance to hurt anyone else or this young girl. I got a response from WIS, which is a news station in South Carolina. The owner's son from the news station lived 15 minutes away from me. So, he came by and we did an interview right there on the spot.

Then the madness started. I began to get calls from everyone because they wanted my story for sweeps week. I got called to do an exclusive interview in Burbank and met a young lady who heard about my story. I didn't know who she was, but we did an Instagram post together and it got millions of views. I was like, what in the world is going on? I had friends calling asking me for Roxy's number. I was like, man, stop playing on my phone. I don't know what you're talking about. They told me to look at my Instagram and I saw that it was Roxy from 106 and Park that I did the interview with and it didn't hit me until that moment. I truly appreciated her support and how brave she was to tackle the issue of equality on her personal Instagram page.

I got called to do an interview for Jake Tapper the same day and they wanted me to go straight to the airport to tell my story. I called my mom and told her what happened and asked her opinion. She thought it was a good idea for me to be able to tell my story and reach out to the young lady who was wrongfully assaulted by the same officer years later.

I took a red-eye and landed in New York around 5 or 6 a.m. I went straight to CNN. I spoke with other guests who were going to be on the show with Jake Tapper. My emotions were everywhere and I kept seeing the video and reliving my horrible experience. I wanted to stand up for minorities because enough is enough and if you don't stand up for something you will die for nothing. The interview started and Jake Tapper made his introduction.

Jake Tapper: This story is brought to you by Carlos Martin in 2007 and Carlos joins us now. Carlos we should point out is an Army veteran and a sergeant who also served in Bosnia. Thank you so much for joining us we appreciate it.

Carlos Martin: Thank you so much sir for having me here.

Jake Tapper: So, um, Carlos what was your reaction when, um, when you learned that this deputy was the man you sued when you see this video?

Carlos Martin: Well, first of all I never had an opportunity to go to court for my lawsuit. My lawyer did me wrong and had the case dismissed without my permission. Um, second, when I saw the video it just reminds me of all the nightmares of what I have been going through for 10 years and if Sheriff Lott would have done the right job the first time, this young lady would never be going through what she is going through right now. You know, because this is what he did to me and my wife. His partner Joseph Clarke beat up Tashiana and slammed her to the ground the same way, handcuffed with her arms behind her back.

Jake Tapper: Now you say deputy Fields confronted you and your wife outside your apartment in 2005 after a noise complaint. You were allegedly playing your music too loudly and you say Fields slammed you to the ground, kicked you, maced you. There was no video evidence although there was photographic evidence. A jury in your civil suit sided with Deputy Fields. What do you say to viewers out there who are skeptical of your story saying, Hey, you had your day in court and the jury's heard the evidence and sided with Deputy Fields.

Carlos Martin: First of all I never had my day in court. The jury's never heard my story. I want you guys to understand that and that Tashiana went to court and when she went to court they didn't even allow me to be a part of her court case. So I'm still looking to have my day in court. I went to the 4th Circuit, and I went all the way to the United States Supreme Court, so I'm still looking for my day in court.

Jake Tapper: Do you think what happened at Spring Valley High yesterday will help you if you do go forward and appeal this case?

Carlos Martin: I think the bigger picture is by me going forward with my case and the young lady going forward with her case it's not just about us but it's about everyone walking the street and it's about everyone's safety.

Jake Tapper: Carlos.

Carlos Martin: It's just not about us but…

Jake Tapper: Go ahead, I'm sorry.

Carlos Martin: It just not about us, it's about protecting our fathers, mothers, brothers and our children.

Jake Tapper: You said in your lawsuit that you believe that race is a factor and why do you think that?

Carlos Martin: Absolutely and he admitted everything in the Internal Affairs report which you can get from my mom, who will be giving you the documentation. Because he's making different comments about I'm glad Johnnie Cochran is dead.

This is the only thing you will be able to see if you Google CNN Jake Tapper Interview with Carlos Martin. I also remember Jake Tapper asking me, "If you could say anything to Officer Fields right now what would you say?" I replied, "I forgive you." What I didn't say is how my forgiveness impacted other people's lives.

After I finished with Jake Tapper it was too early to go to my hotel room and it was raining cats and dogs. I walked around New York looking for Diddy or 50 Cent to tell them my story but I couldn't find them. I was lost in

New York so I decided to call my friend Cameron Gantt from Xbox because he'd been there before. I told him I was in New York and I just finished an interview with Jake Tapper and I was looking for different outlets for me to speak about my circumstance.

I took Ubers to Fox, ABC, NBC, etc., and couldn't get anymore help. He told me to go to the Breakfast Club or Hot 97. It was an amazing and simple idea, but I'm definitely grateful he took the time to help me out. I called an Uber and went to the hottest radio station in America and tried to speak with someone from the Hot 97 crew, but security wouldn't let me in. It was around 5 or 6 p.m. There were a lot of employees going home. I spoke to a majority of the people going home and asked them could they help me get a radio interview with Hot 97.

I was soaked and upset so I decided to leave, but I felt like GOD told me to go back one more time. I went back and there was this gentleman smoking outside and he started talking about the Hot 97 crew and the case that happened with the little girl from Spring Valley. I overheard and spoke to him immediately and told him that I was the soldier who was wrongfully beaten up by the police and I just did an interview on CNN with Jake Tapper. I also showed him what I posted on CNN ireport.com and told him that they flew me out for the day and I fly out tomorrow. He tried to get me in the building but they still wouldn't let me get in to go upstairs.

Finally, someone informed the HOT 97 crew that I was downstairs and I met Nessa. She told me that they just got done discussing the Spring Valley assault. She told me that she would love to interview me. So she asked me to give her 10 minutes to set up so we could go live on the radio. I was patient and excited that I would finally get to tell my story on the radio because I really wanted to reach out to this young lady because we could understand each other's pain from being assaulted by the same officer.

Nessa brought me in to do the interview. I was so grateful. At the time I didn't know that she was dating Colin Kaepernick, who I had previously done security for when he was in a club in San Jose.

Nessa: Hot 97! Where hip-hop lives. Hanging out with Nessa, Carlos Martin. Not a lot of people might know about you because most of the time, when they see Hot 97, they see an artist. You know, celebrity wise. Who are you and why are you here today?
Carlos Martin: Well, I'm a retired United States soldier. But the reason why I'm here is because

I want to build a bridge between police brutality and the public.

Nessa: Now, let's talk about that because obviously you know Ben Fields, who has been all over the news.

Carlos Martin: Correct.

Nessa: OK, now he was the resource officer at Spring Valley High School. The video that's been circling all over the place. The video that's out there about the young girl being pulled out of her chair. Now, you've had an encounter with this man.

Carlos Martin Correct.

Nessa: OK, now explain that situation so that we are aware of why you are even speaking about this.

Carlos Martin: Well, what's so crazy is 10 years ago. He actually beat up me and my wife or ex on the same day. Which is just totally ironic and so what happened to me was I was coming back home from Fort Jackson, South Carolina, where I was stationed at Moncrief hospital. I lived about four miles away from the base. But the fact that it happened off the base so the Army couldn't help me. And actually, the Army turned their back on me once they found out about the situation. The situation was I lived in Quail run and Quail run is shaped like a big rectangle or a big square you would say. And so, when you insert the parking lot it's a rectangle. So the officer was already there. What we found out was that he was there looking for a white male flashing little kids. I drove behind the officer as we entered in my parking lot and in a rectangle eventually we were going to become parallel. So we acknowledged each other. I gave him my head nod or whatever else and I went in my parked my car. I got out my car and I walked to my door to put the keys in my door,next thing you know I hear a car peel off and the officer started running towards me. Which happened to be Benjamin Fields. He's like, Hey, you! Hey you! Come here! Come here! I'm like, OK, how can I help you sir? He was like, I'm out here for a noise violation. I was like, Well it couldn't be. I just got there and the officer asked for my license and registration. I gave my license and registration but the problem was I lost my picture license in Germany where I was serving. I handed them the paper license from Alaska, which is a still a legal document for driving until they see you your picture license or whatever else.

Nessa: OK.

Carlos Martin: So when he saw the picture license, he was like, Well, what the hell is this? And I was like, Dude, if you just calm down, because he's been extra aggressive. I have

German tags on my car. You see I'm in uniform
and I just got back from Germany.

Nessa: Oh, you were in uniform.

Carlos Martin: Oh, absolutely. He beat me up
in my military uniform. So uh, he says what
the hell is this? And I'm like dude if you just
calm down. He was like you will not address
me as dude. I'm a Richland County officer of
the law. I was like you address me by Hey you.
He was like well, that's because I don't know
your name. I was like well, I don't know your
name either? You know, next thing you know
he slams me to the ground. He starts punching
on me, kicking on me and everything else. So I
curl up to protect myself or whatever else. So I
have an internal affairs document backing up
what I'm telling you. He starts making all these
racial comments about how he's glad Johnnie
Cochran is dead. I'm nothing but another
notch on his belt. How he's gonna ruin my
career. So he's making all these racial
comments that is documented. Um, then he
takes out a can of mace and he uses a whole
can of mace on me. Because it didn't bother me
like a normal civilian. He actually became
more violent. He started kicking me and kneed
me in my stomach or whatever else. The crowd
begins to draw. He sees my wife at the time
taking pictures of him. He panics, right? He
gets on the radio and he calls out some type of

code: Help! Help! Help! Like he was in serious distress. When it was nothing but women and children around him. So within three to five minutes, you got eight cop cars or whatever else. I'm not sure but I know it's eight officers but I'm not sure how many police cars it was. They come to the scene within three to five minutes. He was like get her black ass. She has pictures of me. So Officer Joseph Clark slams my wife into another car. She drops her cell phone. He handcuffs her. Now, she's already detained. He picks her up by her arms while they're behind her back and slams her into the ground face first. Now, imagine your wife or your loved one getting beat up and you're helpless and there's nothing you can do to protect her. As a man, as a soldier, just as a human being, period.

Nessa: Absolutely.

Carlos Martin: And then you have to sit there and watch your queen be disrespected like that. When the female officer was on the scene they didn't even allow the female officer to search her. Officer Joseph Clark ran his hands up and down my wife and I couldn't do nothing about it. So after this we get out on bail. I go back to my unit. I tell my unit what happened to me. Now, mind you at this time I was a soldier for months. Soldier of the quarter. I was an MVP for winning trophies. I was outstanding soldier for my unit.

Nessa: Thank you for serving.

Carlos Martin I appreciate that.

Nessa: Our country. Thank you.

Carlos Martin: But what's so crazy is, if I can go out and fight people who I don't know in foreign lands for laws that I believe in for my country that I love, what happens when we come back home? So that's why I entitled this whole thing A War on Friendly Grounds because it seems like I'm fighting more over here than I am in a place that I don't even know for what reasons. I don't even know why?

Nessa: What you mean titled? You titled what?

Carlos Martin: The CNN document that I wrote a long time ago was titled A War on Friendly Grounds.

Nessa: So this is not you coming out of nowhere to discuss this.

Carlos Martin: Absolutely not. The Army turned their back on me. I got flagged. They illegally tried to send me to Korea. I had all the documents proving this. I was a medical record soldier. I worked in the hospital so the same people that I filed congressional on congress with -- I wrote the White House -- was the same people in charge of my med board. They denied me surgery. They put I got out the Army on a medical discharge. I went to the NAACP. I went to the Rainbow PUSH. I went to the Urban League. None of these people wanted to help me because we weren't funding them.

Nessa: In light of everything that's going on. You've had an encounter with Ben Fields, who got fired.

Carlos Martin: Correct.

Nessa As deputy in South Carolina.

Carlos Martin: What's so crazy is after Ben Fields beat me up. The reason why he is at the school is because of what he did to me and that's how me and the young lady are in correlation. He would have never been at the school if Sheriff Lott did what he was supposed to do in the first place. He should have been fired when he jumped me in my military uniform and my wife. He should been fired then but he wasn't fired. He got sent to Spring Valley High School where this incident occurred with this young lady. The reason why I'm here is, one, I want to reach out to the young lady who this happened to because now she faces the same nightmares that I've been living for 10 years.

Nessa: Yeah.

Carlos Martin And I just want her to know that she's not alone but at the same time I've been doing a lot of Facebook posts. And man some of the comments that people say are so malicious. Oh, Officer Fields should die. Oh, it's a good thing that the young lady got her butt whipped on both sides of the pole. Well, all officers aren't bad.

Nessa: Absolutely.

Carlos Martin: You know what I mean and that people have the misconception because one person did something wrong. That means everybody like that.

Nessa: That's not the case.

Carlos Martin: But my problem is we have a lot of good officers out there. You guys know who the bad officers are but we have this thing called snitching. Well, how many people are losing their lives because you don't want to tell the truth about who don't need to be in that department?

Nessa: Right.

Carlos Martin: But it works the same way in the public. You don't want to tell the truth about who the drug dealers are in your community or who the thugs are in your community, but you complain about your community. Well, you guys keep saying the wind got no voice to stand up then I'll be that voice to stand up. I'll take that platform, I'll take that light. I don't give out my phone number on Facebook. I've received so many crazy calls from so many different people but if it's enough to bless this young lady, to help her get her smile back, then it was all worth it. Like honestly, I don't even know how I got in your building.

Nessa: Right, this story is really crazy. Like literally we're doing our show and all of the sudden I don't know who ran in here.

Carlos Martin: I don't even know his name.

Nessa: Yeah, Melvin's part of the afternoon show mellow and he you know. Everyone ran appeared there like Nessa because I posted the video up and I said what is wrong with our society nowadays.

Carlos Martin: Right.

Nessa: So when this was brought to my attention that you were here, I was like, why? What are the chances? Now, I also question what was your motive being in New York?

Carlos Martin: Right.

Nessa: So you're here because you actually had to do a piece with CNN.

Carlos Martin: Yeah, the morning show. I just did that.

Nessa: OK, so you did that earlier today?

Carlos Martin: Yes ma'am, they flew me out from Burbank to New York. I didn't want to waste the opportunity while I was here in where there's so many different people I could try to reach and tell my story. I tried to go to

Fox. I couldn't get in touch with nobody. I tried to go to NBC. Couldn't get in touch with nobody. A friend said why don't you try Hot 97. And you know I did a challenge to President Obama, LeBron James, everybody who do Black Lives Matter, All Lives Matter, everybody who did the Million Man March and here's my question. If you go to the gym one time out of the year are you gonna get in shape? So how do we expect to make a change with the problem this big and we only do it in one time of year? I challenge you guys if we can do bucket challenges and all these other stupid challenges. To walk with me on this walk of equality.

Nessa: What would you like to see because I think this is important to hear this because obviously everyone's going to go right back to the obvious, the race situation?

Carlos Martin: Right.

Nessa: Right. You served our country.

Carlos Martin Absolutely, 10 years.

Nessa: You have no problem with others being, you know, different races?

Carlos Martin: Not at all.

Nessa: This isn't about this for you.

Carlos Martin: Not at all.

Nessa: This is… what is this about?

Carlos Martin: America needs to look at the mirror. It's 2015 and we're still talking about race because that's all it is, invisible lines of hate. So my goal is to bridge the gap between the public and the police. There's a difference between being a police officer and a bully. When you're being a police officer you're following your training. When you go outside your training, you turn into a bully. Officer Fields just turned into a bully because even sheriff Lott said we don't train police to act like that. You guys can see that the building is on fire and be like man that's terrible but you don't know how the people feel that's inside the building while the building's on fire. And so what I want you all to understand is, if I can forgive Ben Fields for what he did to me.

Nessa: And you do forgive him?

Carlos Martin: Absolutely, you know why? Not for him but for me. Because if I didn't I would hold on to all this hate.

King Louie: If you had a chance to speak to Ben Fields would you? And if you would what would you say to him?

Carlos Martin: Absolutely, I would want to look him in his eye and tell him I forgive him. And I'm gonna pray for you man.

King Louie: When you saw the classroom like not reacting. The way you would expect a person to react if they saw like a classmate or somebody. Do you feel like it's just the culture of South Carolina or down south?

Carlos Martin: No, I think that's America wideness. It's sad that we become so detached from each other.

King Louie: So what are some of the steps that you think should be done to make this happen?

Carlos Martin: Man, absolutely. I think all officers should have body cameras on them. From start to finish. So that way people can't say, well you don't know what happened before this video took place, right? Also remember when you played sports and you didn't get a play right? What do you do? You practiced it over and over again. So I think they should have ethics and sensitivity training for police officers, how to deal with the public. But on the flip side of that, I think the public should have classes available to them on the laws and how to handle police officers when encountered. That way both sides know their rights.

Nessa: I think obviously right now there's no trust.

Carlos Martin: None at all.

Nessa: None. Talks are out the window.

Carlos Martin: Well, the problem is this, right? We live in the microwave generation where everybody wants everything now. We live in a generation where kids are having kids. How do you expect things to happen? We don't have leaders that want to stand up and be leaders. We have teachers who have to call a police officer when they're the ones are supposed to be in charge of the classroom. We got to get back to the basics, you know. And that starts with love that starts with how to treat your child at home. You know it's not my job to raise your child. It's your job.

Nessa: Absolutely.

Carlos Martin: You know what I'm saying and stop blaming people when your child does wrong and correct your child. You know what I mean?

Nessa: Right.

Carlos Martin: We got to be willing to put in the work to find good mentors.

King Louie: And that kind of leads me into how do you feel about the Black Lives Matter and do you think it's actually being, um, do you actually think it's doing something out here?

Carlos Martin: I get it, right? But if we go back in the days where we had slavery and everything else when Martin Luther King walked in Selma and the movies and everything else. If you look at that Selma video, was all of that black people? I don't think so. I mean we can go deeper, we can go up to Malcolm X.

Nessa: Yeah.

Carlos Martin: Malcolm X was a Muslim. Malcolm X was all about black people and everything else, right? What happened when he went to Africa and he learned the truth? Muslims just aren't all black, they're all different shades.

Nessa: And he was praying next to those who looked white and Asian and that's what made him come back to America and say it's not about color. It's about the system.

Carlos Martin: Exactly.

Nessa: That's the problem

Carlos Martin: And the problem is the system don't want to be fixed. That's why they killed Malcolm. Anybody that speaks truth about bringing us together has always had their life taken.

Nessa: Do you worry about your life being taken for speaking about this?

Carlos Martin: You know, so funny. I've had so many conversations. You better watch what you say. You know what? We all gonna die one day and if I die I want to die for something. You know what I'm saying. If I gotta die for something. I'm here for a reason and I asked my mom of this. Why wasn't I Trayvon Martin? Why wasn't I Mike Brown? Why we're not the Fruitvale? You know, all these different things that happen, right. To be at this moment.

I don't even know how I got into your office right now. To be in this moment.

Nessa: It was meant to be.

Carlos Martin: Someone has to be the light and I'm just nobody trying to tell everybody about somebody who can love them. I just want to bring love back to the world. You know me so don't look at me as if I'm better than anybody else. I don't think I'm all of that. I'm so humbly grateful to be in this position. But this is 10 years of consistency of not giving up on something that happened to me a long time ago to be in the position I am and I'm not scared.

Nessa: Did it surprise you when you heard that Ben Fields was involved in this situation?

Carlos Martin: It didn't surprise me because you can only bury the truth for so long.

Nessa: Absolutely.

Carlos Martin: Because at the end of day, what I want America to understand is death ain't got no color. Death ain't got no race. Death don't care. So why do we keep putting this race issue and making it bigger than death?

Nessa: We really all need to come together and realize that it's the system that's the problem.

Carlos Martin: Exactly.

Nessa: It's pitting us against one another when really we need to come together.

Carlos Martin: Exactly. Now you got it we're not fighting each other. We're fighting the system.

Nessa: Right, anything else because I want this to be a platform for you to voice you know something that obviously has haunted you for 10 years.

Carlos Martin: I would love to have my day in court, rightfully so.

Nessa: What would you like to happen in court or what would you...

Carlos Martin: I would like a fairly fair lawsuit trial.

Nessa: OK.

Carlos Martin: Where all the evidence is what it is.

Nessa: Against Ben Fields.

Carlos Martin: Absolutely, and Richland County. I would like to fix the problem with the NAACP, the Rainbow PUSH, the Urban League, all these organizations that say they're there. I'm not saying every organization was like that. Just the ones that I dealt with in South Carolina. But on a grand scale I would like to ask everybody this question. If you died today, would you get an A plus on life's report card? Because everybody doesn't wake up to see tomorrow. If you died today, would you get an A-plus on life's report card? If not, and you're blessed to see tomorrow. You better live like this is extra credit because tomorrow's not promised. I just want to take the time to thank Nessa, King Louie and especially Malcolm who blessed us with this amazing opportunity for an interview. I'm so grateful to Hot 97 for blessing me to tell my story.

After I finished the interview with Nessa I did more interviews with WBLS' Jameer Pond and That's Enuff with Unique. I truly appreciate both of them sharing their platforms and their fan base with me because the topic does affect all of us. I know in life we can look over things until it's knocking at our door. Nessa, Jameer and Unique, thank you from the bottom of my heart, thank you. If you Google WBLS interview with Carlos Martin you will be able to watch my interview with Jameer and if you Google That's Enuff interview Carlos Martin you will be able to watch my interview with Unique.

No one is perfect so during the interview I talked about Black Lives Matter. Just because they are saying Black Lives Matter doesn't mean they are being disrespectful to other races. The same way we have breast cancer awareness, etc. It's not that breast cancer awareness is more important than anything else going on in our society. I didn't fully understand but I'm man enough to own up to my mistake. Black Lives Matter is an important group and I'm grateful for everything they do. I believe we need to also use this powerful platform to address multiple topics (i.e. black on black crime, family members touching children, especially young girls in the household, etc.).

Brothers, we have to do a better job policing each other and holding each other accountable for our shortcomings. I'm just as guilty. We have to start looking at that star player in the mirror and stop lying to ourselves to create a wave of change. We don't have to look for a leader when we already have it in our own DNA. We have to be willing to pull the weeds out of our own garden if we want to see the results we claim we want. Responsibility is a powerful tool, but to me it only means the ability to respond. This means we have to get up and stop being lazy or sitting in our mental prison to walk in our destiny.

After I left Hot 97 and I went back to the Empire Hotel, I thought about this quote GOD gave me: "What makes a rainbow beautiful, is it not the diversity of colors? Well, if that's true, is mankind's weakness trying to make one color better than the next? If that happens, is it still a rainbow? I think not! So why are we destroying something, that GOD made beautiful, with invisible lines of hate?" I shared that with the fan base during the interviews, but I was just contemplating on why are we so divided?

I flew back to Burbank the next day. I went on YouTube to watch the interviews and read the comment section to see what people thought about it:

STARS Ave angels: "My G. you're in the military and you let a cop beat you up?
Haha."
MissDAdolph said: "We some forgiving and praying slaves man. We sweep
everything under the rug. Meanwhile, Mexicans are forcing government to treat
them fair and equally. Jews are collecting reparations. Everyone but us praying
forgiving people. SMH."

I received phone calls and death threats. I got everything under the sun. I had people who agreed and understood where I was coming from. I had people who called and said they were ready to riot. It was just so much to take on at one time. I was asked if I was going to be an actor or an activist. I'm fighting for 100% of my VA benefits. My point is, people have to be very careful with their verbal bullets that they throw because it does affect people. Now if I would have taken a gun and shot everyone up, the point of my message would have been lost. The opportunity to create a better future would have been gone along with it.

Forgiveness is not about the other person as much as you think. It's really about yourself. While other people are free enjoying their life, you walk around taking out your frustration on the wrong person. Maxine Waters said, "I'm reclaiming my time." That was a powerful statement. I think, as minorities, we need to take note of her message and take it to the next level. We need to reclaim our families, neighborhoods, finances, unity, and standards.

Chapter 11

The Power of Choice

This is what I chose to do but, honestly, that may not work for everyone. What works for me is having my family because I was able to talk about it. I knew they couldn't understand, but it allowed me to relieve some of the frustration. Listening to motivational speakers like Les Brown, Byron Nelson, Eric Thomas, and allowed me to understand that someone has it worse than you and respecting what they went through.

Activism is not just sitting around doing nothing. That is why I did the radio interviews, spoke about it on television and reached out to the young lady's family. I'm writing this book despite all of my own fears I created in my mind and the reality of living in America. My girlfriend, Ashli, has been such a driving force that inspired me. Honestly, I can't thank her enough for her love and support. Some days I didn't want to get up to complete this book because of frustration. Ashli would push me beyond what I wanted to do. We have a choice to police ourselves and be responsible for our decisions and the context on how we look at things.

You should surround yourself with people who will tell you the truth and not just people who make you feel good. People always ask me, what can I do to fix police brutality? There are different examples in the world where people understand the power of choice. Colin Kaepernick took a stand against the NFL and America for equality and injustices against minorities. He didn't have to take a stand for anything because he was already living a life that most people dream of. He exercised his power to make a difference. He was backed by a strong woman, Nessa, who supported him through this difficult time. Nessa was the host who interviewed me on Hot 97. Kaepernick created the *Know Your Rights Program* to prevent police brutality.

If a police officer is found guilty of abuse, they should be charged as a civilian. We can follow the same blueprint as sexual harassment training for companies and corporations at all levels. I believe road cops need breaks from being on the road too long because they become desensitized. For example, a nurse on her first day at work wants to give the best care to all of her patients. After doing the same job over and over again she loses her love after not being appreciated.

One of our greatest tools, as people, is communication and unity. How can we have positive controversy? What I mean by that is how can we peacefully come together to talk about difficult issues that makes society better. How do we address the elephant of white privilege?

I was talking about police brutality to my Jewish friend Illan. I asked him if he was aware of the history of police officers and the slave patrol. Their job was to catch runaway slaves and bring them back to the plantation. During this process Blacks were raped and murdered. How can we weed out racism if its birthplace is America? Illan was attending UCLA to become a lawyer and I was interested in his perspective regarding police brutality in America. He said something that I believe is very powerful because everyone is not racist. Illan said I want to tell you I'm sorry, but I feel like I would be disrespecting you. I will never face what you go through on a daily basis as a Black man because of my White privilege that I was born with but didn't ask for.

How do we fix this together? I had to sit with that for a second before I spoke. I shared with Illan, he just took one of the biggest steps you can take. Having an open and honest conversation about the differences you and I face. As a minority, we encounter different conditions that most White people would never endure. We have to raise our children by different standards because of racism and the power system in America. Most minorities tell their children things like this before they leave the house: know your rights, put your hands up, turn your music down, pull up your pants, speak in low tones, and control your emotions.

No matter what a black man's lifestyle is in America, we can't escape racism. When I ask my white friends about America's double standards their response is they don't have to worry about those issues when they leave their home. I mean, look at how TV shows, movies, radio, social media portray minorities. When foreigners come from different countries they assume that all blacks are this way. The system we live in feeds us negativity. We have become so desensitized that when we see a police shooting it no longer bothers us. We would rather rant and rave on social media about a peaceful protest. I mean, look at how terrible the Las Vegas shooting was and how many people lost their lives. Where are all the same people who have so much negative energy? Why are they not burning jerseys and all of the other crazy things people come up with?

Colin Kaepernick took a knee and people were outraged to the point President Trump even tweeted about him. I believe the NFL owners talked about it and how it would affect their pockets. I believe they called it protecting the NFL Shield. The owners joined together and took a knee on the field. So, why wasn't that okay when Colin Kaepernick did the same thing? I guess we can't let the inmates run the prison. What is the precious flag supposed to represent? Colin Kaepernick went as far as to ask a soldier how he can take a stand without disrespecting the military. It was so bad Madden 19 bleeped Kaepernick's name out like it was a curse word. They later gave a weak apology and put his name back on the game.

Despite all of the adversity Colin faced, he still believed in his power of choice. He followed up by putting his money where his mouth was. Nike even came out to support equality and justice for all. What does the world do? People started burning all of their NIKE products! So, it's okay to burn things and rant and rave over social media but it's not okay to take a knee peacefully. I personally feel it was a huge moment that got passed over because of a price tag. How many white players were willing to take a knee for the greater good of America? I personally want to thank you for the risk that you took, but the difference is none of you lost your jobs. Being a minority, we face different challenges because of the color of our skin on a day to day basis.

What is the price tag for equality? How much does it cost to stop being wrongfully shot by the police? As a soldier I'm not putting my life on the line for the flag. We are putting our lives on the line for what the flag is supposed to represent for our families. The flag claims it represents liberty, freedom and justice for ALL. Are we living in a nightmare of lies if there is no equality? Are soldiers putting their lives on the line in foreign lands just to come home to family members being murdered? I find it so funny when society changes the narrative of the protest and try to make it about the flag. America claims they love veterans, but have you noticed most homeless people in America are the veterans you claim to love?

I find it so disrespectful to hide racism behind the veterans who fought for our freedom. Do you know how many veterans don't receive benefits they are entitled to? Do you know how long it takes for veterans to be seen at the VA hospital? I was wrongfully jumped by the police in 2005 and it took over 10 years to finally get my 100% retirement. Personally, I still haven't received all of my back pay from the VA. I'm still waiting on the medical review board to approve the rest of my back pay.

One day out of the year we have Veterans Day. Restaurants offer you a free meal but it's from the **special** menu instead of the **entire** menu. Most places don't even offer a military discount to veterans, and the ones that do only offer 10% off. Veterans don't receive the health care they are entitled to by the military because the VA system is so backlogged. Oftentimes, by the time you receive the care, you're not alive to use the benefits.

It's a War on Friendly Grounds right here in America while we cry out, let's make America great again. HOW, AMERICA? You don't want the answer because every time someone asks the question, how should Colin Kaepernick protest? You don't have a response. If you did have the answers or a different way to protest, why aren't you doing it?

Here is a question for the justice system because I want to know if it works both ways. If I go to court and they ask me why I ran and my answer is because I feared for my life, would I be justified? When we go to court why is it that the police are the only ones who can say they fear for their lives? How are you supposed to protect me if you fear me? How is it that we see on TV or social media the wrongful killings but we are not entitled to fear for our lives? Why can't we fear the badge if it's abused by corrupt police officers? How can you sit still and be compliant when you see that people are still being wrongfully shot? Why do you fear me because of the color of my skin?

People say we need to forget about slavery! Okay, let's say we forget about slavery. Would you forget that I'm Black and a person just like you? Botham Jeans was wrongfully shot in his home, yet we talk about burning Nike shoes. Trump would rather tweet about Nike sales instead of tweeting about the injustices in America. My mom used to tell me that we are a reflection of our leadership. You can tell when you have a good leader by looking at his followers.

President Trump, congrats on becoming President because it's something that only 45 men in America have accomplished so far. I have a question for you, Mr. Trump. When has it been okay to go into someone's home and take their daughter, son, brother, sister, mother or father and tell them to live the American dream? You were also on national TV and called NFL players sons of bitches and said if they can't respect the flag they need to get out of this country. Do you feel that same way about the several White officers who wrongfully jumped me in my military uniform or is it just for the minorities?

Does America have PTSD or are there just good and bad people on both sides? Why do we have so many mass shootings in

America? There is a flaw in the system. What are we going to do to make America great for everyone for once?

For Speaking Engagements, Book Signings, Appearances, and Interviews,

Contact:

CARLOS MARTIN
carlos.martin112@yahoo.com
408-466-8238
Instagram: Cluv1121
Facebook: Carlos Martin